Serverless on Kubernetes with Knative

Unlocking the Power of Serverless on Kubernetes

Pradeep Loganathan

https://pradeepl.com/

February 19, 2025

*Dedicated to Sundari, Ashwini & Abhinav,
for inspiring me to reach beyond.*

Serverless on Kubernetes with Knative

by Pradeep Loganathan

ISBN: [978-1-7636129-0-7]

First Edition: February 19, 2025

Cover Design: Pradeep Loganathan

Typesetting: This book was typeset using LaTeX.

Publisher: TheThinkTank Publishing

Website: https://pradeepl.com/

Disclaimer:
This is a technical book intended for educational purposes. While every effort has been made to ensure accuracy, the author and publisher make no warranties, express or implied, regarding the completeness or applicability of the content. The author and publisher disclaim any liability for any direct or indirect consequences arising from the use of this material.

Contents

Contents

Preface

Have you ever found yourself drowning in infrastructure configuration just when you wanted to focus on building your application logic? Are you frustrated by unpredictable costs that spike with every traffic surge? Do you wish you could release new features faster without the fear of breaking your entire system?

Serverless computing offers a way out of this complexity. It's a paradigm shift where infrastructure fades into the background, letting you zero in on code that delivers value. Scalability becomes automatic, and you pay only for the resources your applications actually use.

This book is your guide to fully unlocking the potential of serverless architectures. We'll dive into the essentials, explore powerful design patterns, and demonstrate how Knative streamlines serverless development on Kubernetes. Whether you're a seasoned architect or a developer eager to make your life easier, this book will empower you to build the next generation of scalable, efficient, and resilient cloud applications. This book explores that aspiration, aiming to make serverless computing not just manageable but enjoyable.

Who Should Read This Book

This book is designed for developers, platform operators, and architects exploring serverless computing or maximizing Kubernetes' potential with Knative. Whether you're new to the cloud-native landscape or an experienced practitioner, this guide aims to enhance your understanding of how serverless architectures can be designed and implemented on Kubernetes with Knative. While no prior experience with Knative is required, a basic familiarity with Kubernetes concepts and cloud computing will enrich your learning experience. Additionally, insights into containers and their orchestration will prove beneficial, though not mandatory, for fully grasping the concepts discussed.

A Word on Cloud Native Applications Today

From the first programming languages, to object-oriented programming, to the development of virtualization and cloud infrastructure, the history of computer science is a history of the development of abstractions that hide complexity and empower you to build ever more sophisticated applications. Despite this, the development of reliable, scalable applications is still dramatically more challenging than it ought to be. In recent years, containers and container orchestration APIs like Kubernetes have proven to be an important abstraction that radically simplifies the development of reliable, scalable distributed systems. Containers and orchestrators empower developers to build and deploy applications with speed, agility, and reliabilitycapabilities that once seemed like science fiction.

Navigating This Book

The book unfolds systematically, introducing serverless computing and its benefits, and exploring Knative's role in streamlining serverless development on Kubernetes.

Part One: Serverless Foundations

This part introduces the core principles of serverless computing, tracing its evolution, benefits, and challenges. We explore the diverse landscape of serverless platforms and how Knative integrates with Kubernetes to simplify serverless application development. Additionally, we dive into foundational serverless architecture patterns, including event-driven design, function chaining, and traffic management strategies, equipping you with the tools to build resilient and scalable applications.

- **Chapter 1: Serverless Fundamentals** Explore the evolution of cloud computing leading up to serverless architectures. Understand the principles, benefits, and challenges of serverless computing, including cold starts, observability, and vendor lock-in. Explore its evolution, core building blocks (FaaS, BaaS, CaaS), and real-world use cases. Learn how Knative bridges Kubernetes with serverless computing, enabling scalable, containerized workloads.

- **Chapter 2: Serverless Platforms and Knative** Explore the diverse landscape of serverless platforms, distinguishing Kubernetes-based solutions like Knative from cloud provider-specific offerings. Understand Knative's role in enabling a vendor-neutral, portable serverless framework on Kubernetes. Learn about Knative's modular design and pluggable architecture, allowing seamless integration with networking, observability, and security tools.

- **Chapter 3: Serverless Architecture Patterns** Dive into essential design patterns for serverless computing, addressing challenges such as scalability, decoupling, and asynchronous processing. Understand how to build scalable, decoupled, event-driven applications using Knative. Apply these patterns to real-world use cases, such as e-commerce and data processing pipelines.

Part Two: Building Serverless Apps - Knative Serving

This part explores how to build and manage serverless applications with Knative Serving. You'll learn how to deploy services, control traffic with routing strategies like canary releases and A/B testing, and integrate service meshes for enhanced security and observability. Finally, we'll dive into auto-scaling techniques, including concurrency-based scaling, scale-to-zero, and optimizations to minimize cold start latency. Learn how to deploy resilient, scalable, and cost-efficient serverless workloads on Kubernetes.

- **Chapter 4: Knative Serving Essentials** Get hands-on with Knative Serving, deploying your first serverless application. Understand the lifecycle of a Knative service, including scaling, traffic routing, and version management. Explore key capabilities such as scale-to-zero, automatic traffic splitting, and rollback strategies.

- **Chapter 5: Advanced Knative Serving** Advance your Knative skills with in-depth topics, including traffic management strategies (canary releases, blue/green deployments, A/B testing).Integrate Knative with service meshes (Istio, Kourier, Gloo) for advanced networking, security, and observability. Explore authentication, mutual TLS (mTLS), and traffic encryption to secure your applications.

- **Chapter 6: Auto-Scaling with Knative** Learn about Knative's auto-scaling capabilities, including request-based, CPU-based, and custom metrics-based scaling strategies. Explore Knatives Pod Autoscaler (KPA) and concurrency-based scaling strategies. Understand scale-to-zero functionality and strategies to mitigate cold starts.

Part Three: EDA & Knative Eventing

Serverless architectures thrive on event-driven systems, enabling loosely coupled services that react dynamically to changes. This part explores Event-Driven Architecture (EDA) and how Knative Eventing streamlines event ingestion, routing, processing, and scaling within Kubernetes.

- **Chapter 7: Event-Driven Architecture Fundamentals** Introduce the fundamentals of event-driven architecture, crucial for building reactive, decoupled systems. Learn how events are managed and processed in a serverless context, and the advantages of CloudEvents for standardization.

- **Chapter 8: Knative Eventing & CloudEvents** Dive into Knative Eventing, exploring how to manage events with CloudEvents. Understand how to configure event sources, brokers, triggers, and channels to build scalable, event-driven applications.

- **Chapter 9: Advanced Orchestration with Knative Eventing** Learn advanced orchestration techniques, including function chaining, failure handling, and schema evolution. Discover how Knative Eventing enables multi-tenant and hybrid environments while supporting robust observability and debugging workflows.

Part I

Serverless Foundations

1

Serverless Fundamentals

... Get the fundamentals
down and the level of
everything you do will
rise.

(Michael Jordan)

The landscape of cloud computing has undergone remarkable transformations, continually adapting to meet the ever-evolving demands
of businesses and developers. Among these innovations, serverless
computing stands out as a pivotal shift, fundamentally changing how
applications are built, deployed, and managed. But what exactly propels

serverless computing into the spotlight, and how does it fit into the broader narrative of cloud development and modern applications?

Serverless computing is revolutionizing application development. Imagine a development model where your applications can scale effortlessly from zero to massive traffic bursts, all while keeping costs aligned with actual usage. Organizations the world over are slashing infrastructure costs, rapidly deploying new features, and relentlessly focusing on innovation by embracing serverless computing. This streamlined approach liberates developers from the complexities of server provisioning and scaling, empowering them to spend their valuable time crafting features that delight users and drive business success instead of wrestling with infrastructure. Developers can say goodbye to delayed feature releases caused by slow server provisioning or prevent unexpected traffic spikes crashing your application.

Imagine a world where you, as a developer, can focus purely on crafting your application's logic without worrying about the underlying infrastructure. A world where provisioning servers, scaling them, and handling maintenance operations are concerns of the past. This is not a far-fetched dream but the reality offered by serverless computing. To tap into this transformative potential, a solid understanding of serverless concepts and principles is essential.

This chapter aims to demystify serverless computing, starting with its core definitions and exploring the benefits and considerations that come with adopting a serverless model. Through this exploration, we'll uncover the diverse applications of serverless computing and introduce Knative, a platform that exemplifies the convergence of serverless computing and Kubernetes, offering a glimpse into the future of cloud-native development. We will do this over the following sections

- Evolution of Serverless
- Definition of Serverless

- ► Serverless Building Blocks
- ► Advantages of Serverless
- ► Serverless Considerations
- ► Serverless Usecases
- ► A Glimpse of Knative

As we embark on this journey, remember that understanding serverless computing is not just about grasping its technical definition but recognizing its role in the broader context of software development and cloud infrastructure. Let's begin by defining what serverless computing truly entails and why it has become a cornerstone of modern application development.

1.1 The Evolution of Serverless

Serverless computing represents the convergence of infrastructure and application architecture trends. It abstracts infrastructure management, originating from the utility computing model of the early 2000s. TThis model proposed the concept of computing resources as a metered service. The launch of Google App Engine in 2008 marked a pivotal shift, laying the groundwork for serverless computing by offering developers platforms to deploy applications sans the direct management of servers.

The defining moment for serverless computing arrived in 2014 with AWS Lambda's debut, pioneering the Function-as-a-Service (FaaS) model. Suddenly, you could write a piece of code, throw it at the cloud, and it would just run when needed. AWS Lambda enabled developers to run code in response to events, eliminating the need for manual server provisioning and maintenance. This innovation spurred a flurry of similar services, such as Azure Functions and Google Cloud Functions, and ignited the development of open-source frameworks that adapted these serverless principles for on-premises deployment. It marked the serverless model's maturation from its utility computing and PaaS origins to the versatile FaaS models we recognize today.

Alongside this infrastructure evolution, applications themselves progressed from monolithic blocks of code to the more modular microservices architecture. Initially, the software development realm favored monolithic architectures, where application components were woven into a single, indivisible unit. Though simple in concept, this monolithic approach hampered scalability and swift development, with large, intertwined applications demanding substantial infrastructure investment and leading to suboptimal resource usage during periods of low activity.

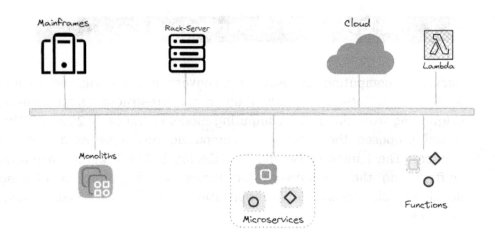

Figure 1.1: Evolution of Serverless Computing

The shift towards microservices architecture represented a significant departure from monolithic design, opting instead for an application structure composed of loosely connected services. This modularity enhances scalability, accelerated deployments, and enabled precise scaling. Despite these advancements, the challenges of server management and associated operational costs lingered. Even with microservices, you still had to think about servers, right? Serverless is where things get really interesting... Serverless takes it a step further, pushing the abstraction of infrastructure to new heights. It allows you to break applications down into even smaller, independently scalable functions. By inheriting microservices based decentralization and removing the onus of infrastructure concerns, serverless computing enables highly scalable, event-driven applications that optimize resource use and cost efficiency. Developers can focus on writing code, safe in the knowledge that their applications scale as needed and incur costs only during active execution.

This ongoing evolution demonstrates a relentless push towards greater efficiency, scalability, and developer focus. It currently represents the cutting edge of cloud-native development strategies.

1.2 Definition of Serverless Computing

Serverless computing is a cloud computing execution model where the cloud provider dynamically manages the allocation of machine resources. Developers write application code as functions, which are triggered by events and run in ephemeral containers. Pricing is based on the actual amount of resources consumed during function execution, rather than pre-purchased units of capacity. This model enables automatic scaling, high availability, and a pay-for-what-you-use pricing strategy, fundamentally changing the game for application development and deployment.

This computing execution model can also be effectively implemented in on-premises environments, where the cloud provider or, in the case of on-premises, the internal platform dynamically manages the allocation of machine resources. Developers write application code as functions, which are triggered by events and run in ephemeral containers, hosted on-premises. In an on-premises scenario, while direct pricing per execution may not apply, the model still emphasizes resource optimization and operational efficiency, enabling automatic scaling, high availability, and effective resource utilization, fundamentally changing the game for application development and deployment. Serverless computing is a key part of the broader cloud-native movement, which emphasizes building and running scalable, resilient, and flexible applications in modern, dynamic environments like the cloud. Cloud-Native approaches often leverage technologies like containers, microservices, and automation to achieve agility and efficiency.

This 'serverless' model signifies that developers are freed from the complexities of provisioning, configuring, and managing infrastructure, regardless of whether the infrastructure is cloud-based or on-premises. In both environments, the responsibility for managing all aspects of the infrastructure, including scaling, patching, and fault tolerance, is handled by the platform. This abstraction empowers developers to focus solely on crafting innovative application features, enabling them to release new functionality with unprecedented speed and agility.

By extending the serverless model beyond the cloud to on-premises environments, organizations can leverage the agility, efficiency, and developer productivity benefits of serverless computing while utilizing their existing infrastructure investments. This comprehensive approach to serverless computing, encompassing both cloud and on-premises scenarios, underscores its versatility and potential to revolutionize application development and deployment across the entire IT landscape.

1.3 Core Principles

At its core, serverless computing is characterized by several key principles that distinguish it from traditional computing models:

- **Abstraction of Infrastructure**: Developers deploy code without concerning themselves with server provisioning, configuration, or management, focusing instead on delivering functionality.

- **Scalability**: Automatic scaling is a hallmark of serverless computing, allowing applications to effortlessly scale up to handle spikes in demand and scale down to minimize costs.

- **Event-driven Execution**: Serverless applications respond to events — be it an HTTP request, a file upload, or a message from another service — enabling reactive, efficient architectures.

- **Statelessness**: Serverless functions are stateless, encouraging simplicity and reliability in application design, though state can be managed through external services.

1.4 Serverless Building Blocks

With the foundational understanding of serverless computing established, it becomes imperative to dive into its key manifestations: Function as a Service (FaaS) and Backend as a Service (BaaS). These models represent the practical embodiments of the serverless concept, each serving unique roles in the development ecosystem. Building on the concept of microservices, serverless computing decomposes applications into smaller, modular units of functionality. These units, often referred to as serverless components, are the building blocks that make up your serverless application. As we explore these services, it's also worth considering the place of Containers as a Service (CaaS) in the broader landscape of serverless computing.

1.4.1 Function-as-a-Service (FaaS)

FaaS is the cornerstone of serverless architectures, offering a way to execute code in response to events without the need to manage the underlying compute resources. This model epitomizes the serverless ideal, allowing developers to focus entirely on their code while the cloud/platform provider handles infrastructure, scaling, and high availability. Developers write individual, short-lived functions that are triggered by specific events (e.g., HTTP requests, database changes, file uploads). The cloud provider handles the execution environment, scaling, and resource management for these functions. FaaS platforms, such as AWS Lambda, Azure Functions, and Google Cloud Functions, enable applications to be highly responsive and cost-effective, scaling automatically to meet demand.

1.4.2 Backend as a Service (BaaS)

While FaaS focuses on the execution of code, BaaS provides a suite of pre-built third-party backend services that are essential for application development. These services, accessible via APIs, include databases, authentication systems, file storage, and more, allowing developers to build feature-rich applications without managing the backend infrastructure. BaaS platforms like Firebase, AWS Amplify, and Supabase simplify the development process, enabling faster delivery of applications with less backend infrastructure code to maintain.

1.4.3 Containers as a Service (CaaS)

While not serverless in the purest sense, Containers as a Service (CaaS) deserves mention for its role in simplifying infrastructure management.

CaaS allows developers to deploy and manage containerized applications through a managed service platform. This model provides greater control over the application environment compared to FaaS and BaaS, bridging the gap between traditional infrastructure management and the serverless model. With platforms like Kubernetes, Azure Container Instances, and AWS Fargate, CaaS offers scalability and flexibility, making it an essential part of the modern cloud-native development toolkit.

Understanding FaaS, BaaS, and CaaS explains the spectrum of serverless offerings available to developers. Each offers distinct advantages and fits different aspects of application development and deployment, collectively covering the breadth of serverless computing possibilities.

1.5 Advantages of Serverless

Serverless computing is not just a buzzword but a transformative approach that offers tangible benefits over traditional and even modern cloud-based infrastructures. These advantages are critical for businesses looking to innovate, scale, and optimize costs in today's competitive landscape.

1.5.1 Cost Efficiency and Scalability

Cost Efficiency: Serverless computing's pricing often ties directly to resource consumption, which can lead to significant savings for applications with variable workloads. Additionally, platforms automatically scale to meet spikes in demand without manual intervention. This elasticity ensures that you only pay for the resources you consume, optimizing cost efficiency.

Automatic Scalability: Serverless platforms automatically scale the application to match the current load, with virtually limitless scaling capabilities. This elasticity means that applications can handle spikes in traffic without any manual intervention or pre-provisioning of resources.

1.5.2 Reduce Operational Management

No Server Management: One of the core premises of serverless is that the cloud provider or the platform operator takes over the responsibility of managing servers, including maintenance, patching, and security. This offloading of infrastructure management allows development teams to focus more on product development rather than operational overhead. This shift in focus empowers developers to innovate faster and deliver new features to users more rapidly.

Streamlined Deployment Processes: Serverless architectures often come with integrated deployment and continuous integration tools, simplifying the deployment process. It can lead to more agile development practices and quicker iteration cycles. This contributes to faster time-to-market and improved developer productivity, which we'll explore in the next section.

1.5.3 Improved Developer Productivity

Focus on Core Product: By abstracting away the infrastructure layer and providing a streamlined deployment process, serverless computing allows developers to concentrate on writing code that adds direct value to their product, rather than managing and operating servers or runtimes.

Enhanced Developer Experience: The serverless model promotes a more streamlined development experience, thanks to managed services for backend tasks, simplified scaling, and built-in high availability. These factors contribute to a development process that's more focused on innovation.

1.5.4 Environmental Impact

Serverless computing can contribute to more sustainable software development practices. By optimizing resource usage and scaling down to zero when applications are not in use, serverless architectures can reduce the energy consumption associated with idle servers, leading to a smaller carbon footprint.

1.6 Serverless Considerations

While serverless computing offers a compelling set of advantages for application development, such as scalability, cost efficiency, and operational simplicity, it is important to consider and address the challenges that might arise. Understanding these challenges ensures that you can make the most out of serverless technologies while minimizing any potential drawbacks.

1.6.1 Vendor Lock-in

Adopting serverless computing often means relying heavily on a specific cloud provider's infrastructure and services (e.g., AWS Lambda, Azure Functions, Google Cloud Functions), which can lead to challenges if you decide to migrate to another provider or deploy across multiple clouds.

Vendor lock-in can restrict your ability to easily switch providers based on factors like cost, feature offerings, or regional availability. You may become reliant on vendor-specific services that could be costlier in the long run compared to alternatives. The ease and availability of vendor-specific integrations may unintentionally influence your architectural choices, potentially leading to less optimal designs in the long term.

To reduce the risk of vendor lock-in, consider using cloud-agnostic serverless frameworks, adopting containerization where possible, and designing applications in a way that abstracts away provider-specific services and APIs. Where applicable, prioritize the use of open standards and technologies (e.g., CloudEvents for event formats, Kubernetes as an orchestration layer). Using open standards reduces your dependency on a single vendor's proprietary implementations. Introduce abstraction layers between your core application logic and vendor-specific services. It allows you to swap out underlying implementations more easily if needed. Frameworks like the Serverless Framework can aid in this. For highly critical applications or those requiring specific capabilities, consider designing your architecture to function across multiple cloud providers. This approach offers greater flexibility but increases complexity and cost. Carefully evaluate the trade-offs between the benefits of deep integration with vendor-specific services against the potential cost of vendor lock-in. Avoid premature commitments to services that might be difficult to switch later. While multi-cloud or hybrid cloud solutions can offer potential strategies to mitigate vendor lock-in, it's important to note that these approaches often come with increased complexity in terms of management and orchestration. Carefully assess whether the resilience and flexibility gained justifies the complexity and expense introduced. There's no one-size-fits-all answer! Striking the right balance between using beneficial vendor features and minimizing lock-in is key.

1.6.2 Reduced Resource Control & Tuning

One of the trade-offs with serverless computing is the reduced control over the computing environment. It can limit the ability to perform detailed performance tuning or to customize the runtime environment extensively. This can make it more challenging to ensure consistent function performance under varying load conditions, as scaling decisions are largely handled by the cloud provider. Serverless might be less suitable for computationally demanding workloads that require specialized hardware or very tight control over resource allocation.

Embrace the best practices for serverless application design, such as optimizing your code for efficiency, leveraging caching, and choosing the right memory and compute resources for your functions. Additionally, consider hybrid architectures that combine serverless with containerized services for greater control when needed.

1.6.3 Cold Start Latency

Cold start latency refers to the delay that occurs when a serverless function is invoked for the first time or after being idle for some duration. It happens as the cloud provider needs to provision a new container, initialize the runtime environment, and load your function code. This latency can impact the responsiveness of serverless applications, particularly for use cases requiring immediate processing. Cold starts have the potential to negatively impact user experience, especially in latency-sensitive or highly sporadic workloads. Unpredictable or substantial cold start delays can lead to customer dissatisfaction or missed service-level agreements (SLAs). Understanding cold starts also helps optimize costs in pay-per-execution models where repeated cold starts can lead to increased costs.

Strategies to mitigate cold start latency include keeping functions warm by invoking them periodically, optimizing code for quicker startup times, and using cloud provider-specific features such as provisioned concurrency or dedicated instances. Some serverless platforms offer the ability to reserve a certain number of pre-initialized dedicated function instances. It ensures immediate request handling with a more predictable cost model but does reduce cost-efficiency benefits for highly variable workloads. Furthermore, smaller function code can help mitigate cold start latency. Where possible, break down complex tasks into smaller, independently-scaled functions. Longer-running functions are more susceptible to cold starts.

Understanding and planning for these considerations are key steps in successfully adopting serverless architectures. By addressing cold start latency, mitigating vendor lock-in risks, and navigating the limitations in resource control and performance tuning, organizations can leverage serverless computing to achieve high scalability, cost savings, and operational efficiency.

1.7 Serverless Use Cases

Serverless computing has become a transformative force in the technological landscape, offering unparalleled flexibility and efficiency for a wide range of applications. Picture this: You're launching an app that could be the next big thing. Serverless computing can power everything from your app's API to real-time data analytics or even enable AI in your app by running model inference. Let's dive into how this looks in the real world. From powering the digital experiences we encounter daily to enabling the cutting-edge innovations of tomorrow, serverless architecture plays a key role in modern software development. Think about the apps you use daily chances are, some of them rely on serverless behind the scenes. This section explores the breadth of serverless applications across current and future state innovative solutions, illustrating its versatility and relevance across various scenarios.

1.7.1 Serverless for the Modern Workhorse

Web Applications and APIs

Dynamic Web Hosting: Serverless functions provide the backbone for dynamic web applications, serving content in response to user requests. Serverless architectures excel at powering the dynamic, interactive, and data-driven experiences demanded by modern web applications. Serverless functions serve as the backend, handling API endpoints, database interactions, user authentication, and real-time updates. This approach allows for highly scalable and cost-effective web hosting, automatically adjusting to traffic volumes without any manual intervention. Serverless functions offer low latency, enabling real-time updates, search results, and other dynamic elements that improve user experience.

API Development and Management: The simplicity and scalability of serverless make it an ideal choice for developing and managing APIs that power modern web applications, mobile apps, and IoT devices. Serverless functions can quickly respond to API requests, making it easier for businesses to build and iterate on their APIs without worrying about the underlying infrastructure. API endpoints powered by serverless functions automatically scale to handle sudden traffic peaks or viral events, ensuring a smooth user experience.

Imagine a social media app with features like image uploading, newsfeed updates, and real-time notifications. Serverless functions could independently handle image resizing, feed updates, notification delivery, and other features. This modular approach allows each component to scale seamlessly based on the specific demand.

Data Processing and Analytics

Streamlined Data Processing Workflows: Serverless architectures excel in scenarios requiring on-demand data processing. Whether it's processing uploaded files, handling streaming data, or performing complex analytics, serverless functions can be triggered by events, process data as needed, and scale automatically to handle peak loads.

Note - Streaming Data
Serverless functions are well-suited for processing individual data items in a stream, analyzing them independently. To track aggregate statistics or trends over time, an external data store would be used.

Real-time Analytics: Leveraging serverless for real-time data analytics allows organizations to analyze data as it's being generated, providing timely insights that can inform business decisions. This is particularly useful in scenarios like fraud detection, social media analytics, and IoT sensor data analysis. Serverless automatically scales to match the volume of data being processed, ensuring optimal resource utilization regardless of workload intensity. There is no need to manage complex data processing clusters; it frees up teams to focus on developing analytical models and data pipelines.

Imagine a marketing analytics platform that needs to process massive clickstream data in near real-time. Serverless functions could be triggered by new data uploads, preprocess the data, compute metrics, and populate dashboards. It offers near-instantaneous results without having to spin up or manage traditional compute clusters.

Microservice Architectures

The decomposition of large applications into microservices finds a natural ally in serverless computing. By encapsulating discrete functionality into independently scalable services, developers can ensure resilience, flexibility, and faster iteration, all while maintaining focus on building value-added features.

1.7.2 Enabling Tomorrow's Innovations

Ever wonder how your smartwatch gets smarter or how real-time analytics can prevent fraud, or how AI-powered medical diagnoses are becoming a reality? Artificial intelligence and machine learning (AI/ML) are undoubtedly at the forefront of these innovations, and serverless computing is a key enabler of this technological revolution. Let's explore how serverless is shaping the future, one event at a time.

IoT and Real-Time Stream Processing

Efficient IoT Device Management: The serverless model is well-suited for IoT applications, where events generated by devices can trigger serverless functions to process data, update databases, or send notifications. This setup allows for efficient management of IoT devices at scale, accommodating the variable and potentially massive volumes of data they generate. Serverless scales seamlessly alongside the number of connected devices or the volume of data being generated, preventing bottlenecks and ensuring system responsiveness.

Scalable Real-Time Stream Processing: Serverless functions can process streaming data in real-time, analyzing and responding to information from sources such as financial transactions, social media feeds, or IoT sensors. This capability supports applications that rely on immediate data processing, ensuring scalability and responsiveness. Serverless functions offer low execution latency and the ability to process events at their source.

Consider a manufacturing facility with sensors on critical machinery that track temperature, vibration, and other performance indicators. Serverless functions could continuously analyze this sensor data. Machine learning models within these functions could detect anomalies or patterns that signal a potential equipment failure. This real-time analysis triggers alerts for preventative maintenance, reducing unplanned downtime and costly repairs.

Machine Learning Inference with Serverless Frameworks

Deploying machine learning models as scalable APIs can be challenging due to unpredictable usage patterns. Serverless frameworks address this challenge by providing a platform for deploying models as functions that automatically scale up to handle bursts of inference requests and scale down to zero when not in use. This makes serverless inference a cost-effective and efficient way to bring the power of your ML models to your users. Additionally, many serverless frameworks offer features like model versioning, monitoring, and A/B testing, simplifying the management of ML models in production environments.

Serverless frameworks such as KServe simplify the deployment and management of machine learning models on Kubernetes. It automatically scales up to handle bursts of inference requests and scales down to zero when not in use, making it a cost-effective and efficient way to bring the power of your ML models to your users. KServe also simplifies the complex process of deploying and managing AI/ML models in a production environment, allowing developers to focus on model development rather than infrastructure management. With features such as multi-model serving, model explainers, and transformer support for pre/post-processing, KServe enhances the serverless ML experience.

Serverless computing offers a compelling approach for building modern, scalable, and cost-effective applications across diverse domains. The use cases presented in this section underscore the adaptability and strength of serverless computing across a variety of these domains. By enabling businesses to build and scale applications more efficiently and cost-effectively, serverless computing is driving a new era of innovation and problem-solving. However, the serverless landscape can be vast and navigating its various tools and frameworks can be a challenge.

The good news is that there are solutions designed to streamline serverless development and management. In the next section, we'll introduce Knative, a powerful open-source framework built on top of Kubernetes that simplifies serverless deployments and operations. Knative provides a standardized approach to deploying and managing serverless functions, offering a bridge between the serverless concepts we've discussed and their practical implementation. We'll explore how these use cases can be implemented and optimized on Kubernetes, further broadening the scope and impact of serverless computing.

1.8   A Glimpse of Knative

Knative represents a significant advancement in cloud-native development, offering a set of middleware components that bridge the gap between the robust orchestration capabilities of Kubernetes and the agility of serverless computing. This section introduces Knative's core concepts, components, and the advantages it brings to serverless application development.

1.8.1 Knative - Bridging Kubernetes and Serverless

Kubernetes is an incredibly powerful system for managing containerized applications, but it often requires a considerable amount of configuration and management to support serverless workloads effectively. Knative addresses this challenge by providing a simplified and consistent developer experience for deploying and managing serverless and event-driven applications on Kubernetes. Knative is an open-source platform built on top of Kubernetes that aims to standardize and simplify serverless workload deployments and operations. It provides developers with essential building blocks and abstractions, making it easier to build, deploy, and manage serverless applications on Kubernetes.

Knative extends Kubernetes by adding key features needed for serverless computing, such as scale-to-zero, eventing infrastructure for building event-driven applications, and a higher-level abstraction for managing serverless workloads.

Knative consists of two primary components that work together to enable serverless development patterns::

- **Knative Serving**: Knative Serving focuses on managing the lifecycle of request-driven (e.g., HTTP) serverless workloads. It facilitates rapid deployment and scaling of serverless applications. It provides features like automatic scaling (up and down to zero), revision tracking, and traffic splitting, enabling developers to roll out updates safely and efficiently.

- **Knative Eventing**: Offers a robust eventing system for composing event-driven applications. It enables developers to build applications that can consume and produce events from a variety of sources(e.g., databases, cloud services, message brokers), making it easier to architect complex, reactive systems. It enables the creation of highly reactive applications.

Knative Eventing leverages CloudEvents, a specification for describing event data in a standard way, enhancing portability and interoperability between services and cloud providers. This standardization simplifies the development of event-driven applications.

Beyond its core components, Knative is part of a larger ecosystem, with support from numerous cloud providers and integration with a wide range of tools and services. Its open-source nature encourages contributions and extensions, allowing the community to evolve and adapt Knative to meet emerging needs.

1.8.2 Why Knative?

Knative is an open-source platform built on top of Kubernetes that aims to standardize and simplify serverless workload deployments and operations. It provides developers with essential building blocks and abstractions, making it easier to build, deploy, and manage serverless applications on Kubernetes.

- **Addressing Vendor Lock-in**: Knative fosters a vendor-agnostic approach. Wouldn't it be great to not feel locked into one cloud provider and have the freedom to move your apps easily? By providing a standard set of building blocks, it reduces reliance on specific cloud provider APIs, enabling portability of serverless applications across different Kubernetes environments.

- **Seamless Integration with Kubernetes**: Knative extends the power of Kubernetes into the realm of serverless. Knative leverages existing Kubernetes concepts and components, making it a natural extension for teams already using Kubernetes. Developers can tap into the rich ecosystem of Kubernetes for monitoring, logging, security, and other operational capabilities offered by the platform.

- **Enabling Hybrid and Progressive Adoption**: Knative allows organizations to gradually adopt serverless patterns. It can work alongside traditional container-based workloads on the same Kubernetes cluster, offering flexibility and reducing the risk of all-or-nothing migrations.

- **Developer Productivity & Efficiency**: By abstracting away much of the complexity associated with deploying and scaling serverless applications, Knative allows developers to focus more on writing code and less on managing infrastructure, leading to increased productivity and faster time-to-market for new features.

- **Open-Source and Community-Driven**: As an open-source project, Knative benefits from the contributions of a vibrant community of developers and companies. This collaboration fosters innovation and ensures that Knative remains at the forefront of serverless computing technology.

Knative represents a pivotal tool in the serverless computing landscape, offering a comprehensive solution for deploying and managing serverless workloads on Kubernetes. By providing a bridge between Kubernetes and serverless, Knative enables more efficient deployment, scaling, and management of applications, making serverless computing more accessible and powerful. Its integration of serving and eventing components provides developers with the tools needed to build scalable, event-driven applications efficiently. As we progress through this book, we will dive deeper into how to leverage Knative's capabilities to build powerful serverless applications, further exploring the practical implications and advanced features of Knative.

1.9 A Serverless Journey

The world of e-commerce presents a unique set of challenges for developers. Customers expect a fast and seamless shopping experience, regardless of whether there are ten visitors browsing your online store or a thousand during a flash sale. Traditional approaches to building web applications often struggle to meet these demands, leading to slowdowns, costly over-provisioning of resources, and difficulties adding new features quickly.

To achieve true business agility, an e-commerce platform must address core challenges: cater to unpredictable traffic patterns, scale efficiently during peak shopping seasons, provide real-time recommendations to users. It should also empower developers by enabling rapid development cycles, and the ability to seamlessly add new features. This book demonstrates how serverless architectures with Knative directly solve these pain points, empowering you to deliver a superior customer experience while maximizing your engineering team's efficiency. Let's embark on a journey where we construct a scalable, adaptable, and cost-effective e-commerce backend piece by piece.

Throughout the following chapters, we'll see how serverless patterns, Knative's capabilities, and careful design choices help us tackle these challenges head-on. By the end, you'll have the knowledge to build your own serverless e-commerce application - or any other ambitious project - with the confidence that it can handle whatever the digital world throws its way. Join me on an adventure to build not just any e-commerce platform, but one that scales effortlessly, dazzles with speed, and evolves on the fly. Ready to see how serverless makes it all possible?

1.10 Summary

In this chapter, we embarked on a journey to explore the exciting world of serverless computing. We began by establishing a clear understanding of serverless, recognizing it as a development model where application logic resides in functions that execute on-demand in response to events. We delved into the compelling advantages that serverless offers, including on-demand scalability, cost-efficiency based on usage, and streamlined development by eliminating server provisioning and management tasks - remember it is like paying for the electricity you use, rather than owning the power plant.

Furthermore, we acknowledged the importance of considering potential limitations in serverless architectures, such as cold start latency, vendor lock-in, and limitations in resource control. By evaluating these trade-offs and applying mitigation strategies, we can make informed decisions on when and how to adopt serverless architectures.

Our exploration extended to a range of compelling use cases where serverless shines, from powering modern web applications and APIs to real-time data processing pipelines and event-driven architectures for the Internet of Things (IoT). These examples showcased the versatility of serverless in addressing diverse application needs and the potential to drive efficiency and innovation.

Finally, we introduced Knative, a powerful open-source framework built on Kubernetes. Knative plays a pivotal role in simplifying serverless development and management on Kubernetes. It offers a standardized approach, reduces vendor lock-in, and allows for a hybrid model where traditional and serverless workloads can coexist. We highlighted its key components (Serving and Eventing) and its role in simplifying the deployment and management of serverless applications.

Remember, serverless is all about simplifying how we build applications - from scaling to keeping those costs down. As we move forward, the insights gained from this chapter will serve as a foundation for understanding the more technical aspects of serverless computing and Knative.

Now that we understand serverless fundamentals, it's time to explore the various platforms that bring these concepts to life. Chapter 2 dives into serverless platforms, comparing cloud provider solutions with Knative's Kubernetes-based approach. We'll explore how Knative leverages Kubernetes to provide a robust and flexible serverless platform. This understanding is crucial for appreciating the full potential of serverless architectures and how they can be implemented efficiently. Ready to see how the leading serverless platforms compare and how Knative stands out? Chapter 2 dives into the details of serverless platforms and the unique advantages of Knative.

2

Serverless Platforms and Knative

The most dangerous
phrase in the language is,
We've always done it this
way.

(Grace Hopper)

Serverless computing has revolutionized application development, but with so many platforms available, how do you choose the right one? Should you go with a cloud-provider solution like AWS Lambda, or a

Kubernetes-based alternative like Knative? What trade-offs do these options present, and how do they impact scalability, cost, and flexibility? This chapter aims to navigate the diverse landscape of serverless computing, highlighting Knative's unique value proposition in this ecosystem. We'll examine Knative's capabilities, its integration with Kubernetes, and its advantages in creating portable and scalable applications. Understanding the available serverless solutions will equip you to make informed architectural decisions for your applications. We'll also introduce a sample e-commerce application that will serve as a practical example through subsequent chapters, demonstrating Knative's capabilities in a real-world scenario. Our journey through this chapter aims to demystify serverless architecture, highlighting Knative's capabilities and its synergies with Kubernetes. You will be equipped to:

- **Grasp** the breadth and depth of the serverless computing landscape, understanding the distinctions and similarities between Kubernetes-based and cloud provider-specific serverless solutions.
- **Appreciate** Knative's unique value proposition, learning how it simplifies serverless application deployment and management by leveraging Kubernetes' inherent strengths.
- Recognize the benefits of portability and open-source innovation offered by Knative, understanding how it enables applications to run across different environments and fosters a collaborative development approach.
- **Identify** Knative's core components and functionalities, including Services, Routes, Revisions, and Configurations, and how they contribute to managing serverless workloads efficiently.
- **Discover** how Knative integrates into the cloud-native ecosystem, seeing its compatibility with other cloud-native tools and services and how it supports building comprehensive, scalable, and efficient applications.

Navigate the challenges of serverless application development, such as managing application complexity, automating scaling decisions, and orchestrating event-driven workflows, and learn how Knative addresses these issues.

2.1 The Serverless Landscape

The serverless computing landscape is rich and varied, offering developers a range of options. Its promise of scalability, cost efficiency, and developer agility, has fuelled a rich ecosystem of platforms and frameworks, each offering unique features and capabilities. This landscape is diverse, comprising several frameworks and platforms that cater to different needs. This diversity, while empowering, can also be daunting. Understanding the strengths and nuances of these solutions is crucial for architects and developers aiming to leverage serverless technologies effectively.

As we navigate this diverse ecosystem, it becomes evident that the landscape is marked by two distinct types of offerings: Kubernetes-based serverless platforms and cloud provider-specific solutions. Each pathway offers unique advantages and considerations, catering to different operational needs and architectural preferences.

On one hand, Kubernetes-based serverless platforms leverage the widespread adoption and flexibility of Kubernetes, offering a more open and vendor-neutral approach to serverless computing. On the other, cloud provider-specific offerings integrate deeply with their respective ecosystems, providing a seamless, managed serverless experience with proprietary advantages.

Understanding the nuances of these choices is crucial for making informed decisions that align with your project's goals and operational constraints. In the following sections, we'll explore Kubernetes-based serverless platforms, highlighting their features, advantages, and how they compare with Knative's approach, setting a foundation to explore the tailored solutions offered by major cloud providers subsequently.

2.1.1 Kubernetes-based Serverless Platforms

Kubernetes has rapidly evolved from its origins as a container orchestration system developed by Google to become the cornerstone of cloud-native application deployment and management. Its emergence as a pivotal platform for serverless architectures can be attributed to its robust ecosystem, scalability, and the community that continually enhances its capabilities. The serverless paradigm, which emphasizes on-demand resource utilization and abstracts away infrastructure management, found an ideal ally in Kubernetes. Early attempts at serverless computing often wrestled with issues like vendor lock-in and limited control over performance and cost optimizations. Kubernetes, with its open-source nature and flexibility, offered a resolution to these challenges, providing a standardized platform for deploying and scaling applications irrespective of the underlying infrastructure.

The rationale behind Kubernetes as an ideal platform for serverless solutions lies in its inherent capabilitiesauto-scaling, self-healing, and load balancingthat align seamlessly with the serverless model of computing. Kubernetes' ability to dynamically manage workloads and efficiently allocate resources ensures that applications can scale to meet demand without manual intervention, a core tenet of serverless computing. Furthermore, Kubernetes' service discovery, secrets management, and native support for CI/CD pipelines enhance developer productivity, allowing them to focus on writing code rather than managing servers.

Kubernetes provides a robust foundation for serverless platforms, blending serverless efficiency and scalability with control, portability, and an extensive ecosystem. It addresses the shortcomings of earlier serverless attempts by eliminating vendor lock-in and providing comprehensive control over application deployment and scaling. As serverless computing continues to evolve, Kubernetes stands as a beacon for innovation, offering developers and organizations a path to harness the benefits of serverless architectures while mitigating its traditional limitations. This has led to it becoming a robust foundation for several serverless platforms, including OpenFaaS, Fission, and Kubeless. Let's outline their key features:

However, leveraging Kubernetes for serverless computing presents its own set of challenges. The operational complexity of managing Kubernetes clusters, configuring networking and storage, and ensuring security can be daunting for teams without dedicated DevOps expertise. Resource management, especially for auto-scaling and scale-to-zero scenarios, requires careful tuning and monitoring. Additionally, the learning curve for Kubernetes can be steep, requiring a significant investment in training and expertise.

This synergy between Kubernetes and serverless architectures has paved the way for innovative platforms built on Kubernetes, which extend its capabilities to provide serverless functionality with additional ease of use and flexibility. By leveraging Kubernetes' robust features, these platforms enable developers to focus on creating business logic while abstracting much of the operational complexity. Among the prominent Kubernetes-based serverless platforms are OpenFaaS, Fission, and Kubeless, each tailored to specific use cases and developer needs. Let's explore their key features:

- **OpenFaaS**: Simplifies the deployment of serverless functions with Kubernetes, offering ease of use and a rich ecosystem. It focuses on simplicity and ease of use. It employs function templates written in various languages and packaged as Docker containers. OpenFaaS provides a Kubernetes controller that automatically provisions pods based on incoming requests, scaling the function instances up or down. Built-in gateways route traffic to the appropriate functions. OpenFaaS offers a robust plugin ecosystem for extending functionality.

- **Fission**: Emphasizes speed and developer productivity, allowing for rapid deployment of serverless functions on Kubernetes. It utilizes serverless functions as Kubernetes deployments. Functions are packaged as container images and uploaded to a registry. Fission's controller watches for new image uploads and automatically creates Kubernetes deployments for them. It also provides built-in scaling mechanisms and integrates with service discovery tools like Linkerd or Istio.

- **Kubeless**: Provides a Kubernetes-native serverless framework that mimics AWS Lambda's model, enabling function execution without manually provisioning underlying infrastructure. Inspired by AWS Lambda, Kubeless functions are deployed as event handlers. Developers write code and define triggers (like HTTP requests or events from other services). Kubeless takes care of provisioning serverless function instances on Kubernetes upon receiving triggers.

- **Knative**: Knative, built on Kubernetes, leverages its underlying features to offer scale-to-zero functionality, automated deployments, and a unified model for serving HTTP requests and reacting to events, encapsulating the essence of serverless computing on a robust, extensible platform. It stands out by offering both serving (request-driven) and eventing models, deeply integrated with Kubernetes and Istio. This combination facilitates complex workflows and enhances developer productivity.

Table 2.1 below provides a comparative overview of the key features and strengths of various Kubernetes-based serverless platforms:

Feature	OpenFaaS	Fission	Kubeless	Knative
Ease of Use	High	Medium	Medium	High
Scalability	Auto-scaling	Auto-scaling	Event-driven scaling	Scale-to-zero
Language Support	Multiple	Multiple	Multiple	Multiple
Integration with Kubernetes	High	High	High	High
Event-driven Support	Yes	Yes	Yes	Yes
Traffic Splitting	No	No	No	Yes
Community Support	Strong	Medium	Limited	Strong

Table 2.1: Comparison of Kubernetes-based Serverless Platforms

While Kubernetes-based serverless platforms offer flexibility and open-source advantages, cloud providers also provide fully managed serverless services with deep ecosystem integration. Now that we've outlined the Kubernetes-based approaches, let's turn to the fully managed serverless services pioneered by major cloud providers.

2.1.2 Cloud Provider-Specific Offerings

Cloud providers have played a pivotal role in the evolution of serverless computing. The genesis of serverless computing can be traced back to the launch of Amazon Web Services' (AWS) Lambda in 2014. AWS Lambda represented a paradigm shift in cloud computingallowing developers to run code in response to events without provisioning or managing servers. This model, termed serverless, fundamentally changed how applications were built and deployed, focusing on event-driven architectures and microservices. Lambda's introduction was not just a technological innovation but also a strategic move by AWS to abstract infrastructure management further, making cloud computing more accessible to developers.

Following the trail blazed by AWS Lambda, other cloud providers quickly recognized the potential of serverless computing and began developing their offerings. Google Cloud Functions, introduced in 2016, and Microsoft Azure Functions, also launched in 2016, followed suit, providing similar capabilities tailored to their respective cloud ecosystems. These services allowed developers to deploy small, single-purpose functions that could be executed in response to various triggers, such as HTTP requests, database changes, or queue messages, further cementing serverless computing's role in modern application development.

- **AWS Lambda**: A pioneer in serverless computing, offering seamless integration with AWS services. Functions are written in various supported languages and packaged as ZIP archives. Lambda manages the underlying infrastructure, including provisioning, scaling, and security. Functions are invoked through Events (like S3 object uploads) or API Gateway requests. Lambda integrates seamlessly with other AWS services for extended functionality.

- **Google Cloud Functions**: Provides a fully managed environment for running serverless applications on Google Cloud. Functions are written in various languages and deployed to Google Cloud Platform. Cloud Functions provide a fully managed environment, handling scaling, infrastructure provisioning, and security. Functions can be triggered by HTTP requests, Cloud Storage events, Pub/Sub messages, or other Google Cloud services.

- **Azure Functions**: Offers tight integration with Azure services, supporting a wide range of programming languages and triggers. Functions can be written in various languages and deployed as code or pre-built containers to Azure. Azure Functions offer a fully managed environment, handling scaling, infrastructure provisioning, and security. Functions can be triggered by HTTP requests, queues, timers, or other Azure services.

While cloud provider-specific offerings provide convenience and ease of use due to their deep integrations, they often lead to vendor lock-in. Knative, in contrast, promotes a cloud-agnostic approach, enabling applications to run on any Kubernetes cluster, irrespective of the underlying cloud provider.

In the next sections of this chapter, we'll look at an overview of Knative, exploring its core components, advantages over other platforms, and how it leverages Kubernetes for serverless deployments.

2.2 Why Knative

In the evolving landscape of serverless computing, Knative distinguishes itself by expertly combining the inherent strengths of Kubernetes with the agility and scalability of serverless architecture. Born from Kubernetes' complex yet powerful orchestration capabilities, Knative simplifies the deployment and management of applications, enabling developers to focus on code rather than infrastructure. It automates critical tasks such as traffic routing for blue/green deployments, auto-scaling to zero to optimize resources, and seamless revision manage-mentall while ensuring applications remain agile and responsive to demand.

What truly sets Knative apart is its commitment to portability and open-source innovation. Designed to run on any Kubernetes cluster, regard-less of the hosting environment, Knative empowers organizations to avoid vendor lock-in, ensuring freedom and flexibility in how and where they deploy their serverless applications. This portability, combined with a thriving open-source community, accelerates innovation and fosters a rich ecosystem of complementary tools and extensions. Knative is not just software; it's a movement towards a more efficient, scalable, and collaborative way of building serverless applications, supported by one of the most dynamic communities in the cloud-native space.

As we appreciate Knative's ability to streamline serverless computing on Kubernetes, it's imperative to dive into the specific challenges it addresses, starting with the manual effort traditionally required in scaling.

2.2.1 The Burden of Manual Scaling

Predicting traffic patterns and manually adjusting pod replicas to match load is time-consuming, error-prone, and often reactive rather than proactive. This can lead to either slow user experiences during unexpected traffic spikes or unnecessarily high costs due to over-provisioning.

Knative automates scaling based on incoming requests, custom metrics, and inactivity, optimizing resource use without manual intervention. This dynamic scaling ensures a responsive application without manual intervention, optimizing resource usage and costs. Beyond the automation of scaling, Knative significantly reduces the operational complexity associated with managing modern, microservices-based applications.

2.2.2 Managing Application Complexity

Modern applications often consist of numerous microservices, distributed APIs, and diverse workloads. Managing configuration, traffic routing, versioning, and the lifecycle of these components directly on Kubernetes can introduce significant operational overhead.

Knative provides a higher level of abstraction, allowing developers to focus on application logic rather than intricate Kubernetes configurations. By defining the desired state of their services, Knative handles the complexities of deployment and management. Another aspect of complexity is the orchestration of event-driven workflows. Knative's approach to this challenge highlights its versatility and power in facilitating seamless, scalable event-driven architectures.

2.2.3 Challenges of Event-Driven Workflows

Building scalable, reliable, and loosely coupled event-driven architectures with traditional tooling often requires custom solutions or intricate configurations. This can hinder development velocity and increase maintenance burdens.

Knative Eventing provides a structured way to create event-driven systems. With concepts like Brokers, Triggers, and Channels, it simplifies the development of reactive workflows that connect distributed components, enabling flexible and scalable architectures.

By addressing these challenges, Knative simplifies the process of building and running applications on Kubernetes. It empowers developers to focus on delivering business value rather than wrestling with infrastructure complexities. Whether you're dealing with unpredictable workloads, intricate microservice architectures, or event-driven systems, Knative offers a powerful toolset for streamlining application delivery and management which brings even more advantages along the way.

Having navigated through the key challenges Knative addresses — scaling, application complexity, and event-driven workflows — it becomes clear why this platform stands out in the serverless ecosystem. This foundation sets the stage for a deeper look into Knative's distinct advantages, further solidifying its position as a leading solution for serverless computing

2.3 Knative's Advantages

Knative stands out as a powerful and versatile serverless framework that addresses many of the challenges developers face when building and deploying modern applications. Knative's unique combination of features, its cloud-agnostic approach, and its focus on developer experience make it a compelling choice for modern application development. Here's a breakdown of why Knative is a compelling choice for the modern application developer:

- **Portability**: Knative offers a cloud-agnostic approach. Applications built on Knative can run on any Kubernetes cluster, whether on-premises or across multiple cloud providers, minimizing vendor lock-in.

- **Control and Flexibility**: Knative builds upon Kubernetes primitives, providing fine-grained control over scaling policies, traffic routing, revision management, and more.

- **Request and Event-Driven Support**: Knative supports both traditional request-response workloads (REST APIs, web applications) and asynchronous, event-driven architectures. This versatility aligns well with diverse application requirements.

- **Growing Ecosystem**: Knative benefits from a rapidly expanding ecosystem of complementary tools and integrations for observability, CI/CD pipelines, and more.

In summary, Knative offers a compelling combination of portability, control, flexibility, and ecosystem support, making it an attractive choice for developers seeking a robust and adaptable serverless framework. Whether you're building cloud-native applications, migrating existing workloads, exploring event-driven architectures, or deploying AI/ML inference models, Knative provides the tools and features to simplify your journey and accelerate your innovation.

2.4 Knative's Core Components

The previous section explored how Knative addresses challenges encountered with traditional Kubernetes deployments. Knative goes beyond simply managing workloads - it provides a higher-level abstraction designed specifically for taking advantage of serverless principles. Let's now understand the core components that make up this powerful serverless framework, with an emphasis on their purpose and how they interact:

2.4.1 Knative Serving

Knative Serving provides the building blocks for deploying and managing serverless, request-driven workloads on Kubernetes. At its core, Knative Serving simplifies tasks such as deployment, traffic routing, scaling, revisions, and management of your serverless applications, ensuring they are always ready to respond to requests. Let's introduce its key components

Services

Services represent your deployable units. Each Service encapsulates the code for your serverless application. Services in Knative are dynamic, automatically managing the lifecycle of your applications, from deployment through updates and scaling. When you create or update a Service, Knative handles the provisioning and scaling of the necessary infrastructure, ensuring high availability and efficient resource utilization.

Routes

Routes in Knative are the intelligent pathways that control how and where your incoming requests are directed. Routes manage the traffic flow to different versions of a Service. Knative's Routes enable:

- **Canary Deployments**: Gradually releasing new versions to a subset of users to minimize risk.

- **A/B Testing**: Experimenting with different versions to determine which one performs better.

- **Traffic Splitting**: Distributing traffic among multiple versions based on defined percentages.

Routes empower developers with the flexibility to test new ideas, roll out updates safely, and manage traffic flow with precision, ensuring the right request reaches the right version of your application at the right time.

Revisions

Revisions are immutable snapshots of your application, capturing the state of your application's code and configuration at a specific point in time. This immutability allows for instant rollbacks and gradual rollouts. Knative enables traffic splitting between revisions for canary deployments, A/B testing, and gradual rollouts. Revisions serve as the backbone for reliable, resilient deployments, offering a safety net that encourages innovation by minimizing the risks of introducing new features.

Configurations

Configurations are the blueprints of your Knative Service, defining the desired state of your application, including its container image, environment variables, and scaling parameters. Whenever you update a Configuration, Knative automatically generates a new Revision, ensuring that your application evolves safely and predictably over time. By altering a Configuration, you communicate your intent to Knative, whether it's deploying a new version of your application, adjusting resource allocations, or modifying environment variables. Knative takes care of the rest, reconciling the current state of your application with this desired state, and managing the transition smoothly and efficiently.

This diagram 2.1 captures the relationship and interaction between the various components of Knative Serving, showcasing how they work together to manage serverless applications efficiently.

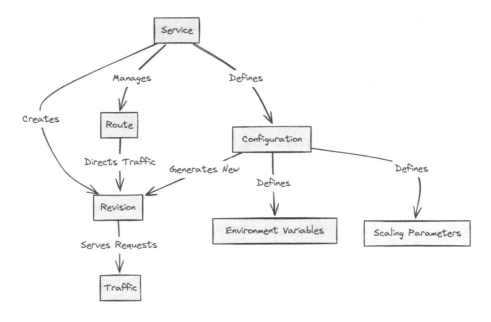

Figure 2.1: Knative Serving

Part II of this book will delve deeper into Knative Serving, exploring how to build, deploy, and manage serverless applications using its core components. By understanding these foundational concepts, you'll be well-equipped to harness the full power of Knative Serving in your serverless journey.

While Knative Serving focuses on efficiently managing and scaling request-driven workloads, Knative Eventing extends this capability to event-driven architectures, enabling applications to respond dynamically to a wide range of events.

2.4.2 Knative Eventing

Knative Eventing is a robust framework designed to enable event-driven architectures within Kubernetes. It simplifies the process of connecting diverse components in a reactive manner, ensuring scalability, reliability, and loose coupling. Eventing facilitates the development of applications that can respond dynamically to a variety of event sources, making it an essential component for building modern, event-driven systems.

Knative Eventing is built on the principles of cloud-native design, offering flexibility and standardization for handling events. Let's look at its core concepts and components, which work seamlessly together to power event-driven applications:

Event Sources

Event Sources are the originators of events in Knative Eventing. They represent external or internal systems that generate events to be consumed by applications. Examples include:

- **HTTP Requests**: Trigger events through RESTful APIs.

- **Messaging Systems**: Events originating from queues like Kafka or RabbitMQ.

- **Database Changes**: Events triggered by updates or modifications in a database.

- **Cloud Services**: Integration with external services such as AWS S3 or Google Pub/Sub.

Knative provides built-in sources and supports custom event sources, allowing developers to tailor integrations to specific needs.

Channels

Channels serve as the backbone for event transportation in Knative Eventing, providing a mechanism to decouple event producers from consumers while ensuring reliable and scalable delivery. They support multiple implementations, including in-memory channels for lightweight, low-latency scenarios and message brokers like Kafka for high-throughput, durable use cases. Channels enhance system resilience by abstracting the event transportation layer, enabling seamless changes without disrupting the producer-consumer relationship.

Subscriptions

Subscriptions define the connection between Channels and event consumers. They specify how events should be delivered and processed by the consuming services. Subscriptions include **Filters** which specify conditions that determine which events are delivered to the consumer. It also allows to specify **Delivery Options** which enable configuration for retries, dead-letter queues, and other delivery parameters. This granularity allows developers to fine-tune the flow of events, ensuring precise and reliable handling.

Brokers and Triggers

Brokers and Triggers work together to facilitate event routing and filtering. Brokers are centralized hubs that aggregate events from multiple sources and route them to the appropriate consumers. Triggers define the conditions under which events are forwarded to specific consumers. Triggers enable advanced filtering based on event attributes, ensuring that only relevant events reach each consumer. This combination of Brokers and Triggers simplifies the creation of dynamic and scalable event-driven workflows.

The diagram 2.2 below illustrates the core components of Knative Eventing and how they interact to enable event-driven architectures within Kubernetes.

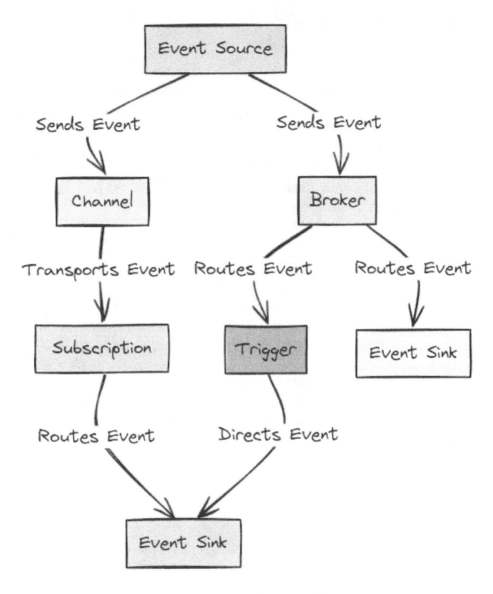

Figure 2.2: Knative Eventing

CloudEvents and Knative

To achieve interoperability and compatibility across diverse systems, Knative Eventing leverages the CloudEvents specification. CloudEvents is a standardized format for describing event data, which simplifies the process of event exchange between different systems by providing a common language for event metadata. Several other systems and services also support the CloudEvents specification, enhancing their interoperability with Knative. Examples include: Kafka, Azure Event Grid, Amazon EventBridge and others.

Benefits of Using CloudEvents with Knative:

- **Interoperability**: CloudEvents standardizes the way event data is structured, making it easier to integrate with various services and platforms that support the specification.

- **Flexibility**: By adhering to the CloudEvents specification, Knative Eventing can handle events from a wide range of sources, including cloud services, third-party APIs, and on-premises systems.

- **Compatibility**: CloudEvents ensures that events produced by one system can be consumed by another, regardless of the underlying technology stack, thus enhancing the portability and scalability of event-driven applications.

How Knative Utilizes CloudEvents:

- **Event Metadata**: Knative Eventing uses CloudEvents to encapsulate event metadata, such as event type, source, and timestamp. This standardization simplifies event handling and processing.

- **Event Routing**: By using CloudEvents, Knative can route events to the appropriate consumers based on their metadata, ensuring that the right components react to the right events.

- **Integration with Cloud Services**: Knative Eventing can seamlessly integrate with cloud services that support CloudEvents, enabling the development of robust, cloud-native event-driven applications.

By utilizing CloudEvents, Knative Eventing ensures that events are handled in a standardized, interoperable manner, enhancing the flexibility and scalability of the event-driven architecture.

Part III of this book will delve deeper into Knative Eventing, exploring how to build reactive, event-driven applications using its core components. By understanding these foundational concepts, you'll be well-equipped to harness the full power of Knative Eventing in your serverless journey.

2.5 Knative in the Cloud-Native Landscape

Knative occupies a strategic position within the cloud-native landscape. Its design philosophy and capabilities are intricately aligned with the principles of cloud-native development, making it a quintessential component for organizations looking to harness the full potential of modern cloud architectures.   It focuses specifically on enabling serverless workloads on Kubernetes. While cloud-native encompasses a wide range of technologies, Knative's strength lies in simplifying the deployment, scaling, and management of containerized applications, offering a more streamlined developer experience for serverless use cases.

Knative doesn't exist in isolation. It complements and integrates with a plethora of cloud-native tools and services, from CI/CD pipelines and observability tools like Prometheus and Grafana to mesh technologies such as Istio. For e.g., It's integration with Istio empowers fine-grained control over network traffic between microservices. When combined with Knative, developers gain advanced traffic routing capabilities like A/B testing, canary deployments, and traffic splitting based on complex rules. This interoperability enables developers to build comprehensive, end-to-end solutions that leverage the best of open-source innovations, ensuring applications are not only scalable and efficient but also resilient and observable.

Beyond its technical capabilities, Knative plays a pivotal role in nurturing a diverse ecosystem of serverless solutions. It sets standards for serverless computing on Kubernetes, encouraging the development of plugins, extensions, and complementary tools. This vibrant ecosystem not only accelerates the adoption of serverless models but also empowers organizations to tailor solutions to their specific needs, fostering a culture of experimentation and innovation. Within the cloud-native landscape, Knative stands as a testament to what's achievable when the community comes together to solve complex problems. By simplifying serverless computing on Kubernetes, it not only makes the technology more accessible but also pushes the boundaries of what's possible, driving the cloud-native movement forward.

Having explored how Knative fits into the broader cloud-native ecosystem, let's look at some emerging trends that will continue to shape serverless computing in the coming years.

2.6 Future Trends in Serverless Computing

As the serverless computing paradigm continues to evolve, several trends are emerging that will shape its future:

2.6.1 Serverless for AI/ML

The integration of serverless computing with AI/ML workloads is becoming increasingly prevalent. While this book focuses on Knative, tools like KServe are paving the way for scalable, efficient ML model deployment, making serverless a natural choice for AI/ML applications.

2.6.2 Hybrid and Multi-Cloud Deployments

Organizations are increasingly adopting hybrid and multi-cloud strategies to avoid vendor lock-in and optimize their cloud investments. Knative's cloud-agnostic approach aligns well with this trend, enabling seamless application portability across different environments.

2.6.3 Edge Computing

Serverless computing is extending to the edge, enabling low-latency processing for IoT and real-time applications. Knative's flexibility and scalability make it well-suited for edge deployments, providing a consistent platform across cloud and edge environments.

2.6.4 Security and Compliance

As serverless adoption grows, so do concerns around security and compliance. Future developments will focus on enhancing the security features of serverless platforms, ensuring robust protection for applications and data.

By staying ahead of these trends, Knative continues to evolve, providing developers with a cutting-edge platform for building modern, scalable applications.

2.7 Summary

In this chapter, we explored the diverse serverless landscape, comparing Kubernetes-based solutions like Knative with cloud provider-specific offerings. We also examined Knative's advantages, its core components (Serving and Eventing), and how it integrates with the cloud-native ecosystem. The next chapter will guide us through the exploration of powerful architectural patterns specifically designed to leverage the unique strengths of serverless architectures with Knative. Understanding these patterns is crucial for leveraging serverless computing's full potential, particularly in complex, event-driven applications. In the next chapter, Chapter 3 — we'll explore the core serverless patterns that showcase Knative's capabilities, illustrating how to build truly powerful and scalable applications.

3

Serverless Architecture Patterns

> ...Design is a plan for arranging elements in such a way as best to accomplish a particular purpose.
>
> *(César Pelli)*

In the evolving landscape of cloud computing, serverless architecture *continues to transform* how we develop, deploy, and manage applications. In previous chapters, we examined serverless fundamentals and introduced Knative, a framework that simplifies building and managing serverless workloads on Kubernetes. With this foundation in place, we can now explore *core design patterns* that help us architect successful serverless applications.

Serverless computing's promise of scalability, cost efficiency, and *infrastructure abstraction* has captivated developers, operators, and enterprises alike. Yet, adopting serverless brings unique architectural challenges: ensuring performance, resilience, and maintainability in highly distributed environments. The key to addressing these challenges lies in applying proven design patterns tailored to serverless.

This chapter provides a comprehensive look at common *serverless architecture patterns* — explaining why they matter, how they work, and when to apply them. By mastering these patterns, you can harness the full potential of serverless computing. You will learn how to:

- ▸ **Understand** why serverless architecture patterns are essential
- ▸ **Explore** key serverless patterns and their practical applications
- ▸ **Recognize** when and how to apply each pattern effectively
- ▸ **Navigate** the selection process, balancing trade-offs and aligning patterns with project requirements

3.1 Demystifying Serverless Design Pattern

Design patterns are the distilled essence of proven solutions to recurring problems in software engineering. Design patterns are essential for maximizing the potential of serverless architectures. They provide a shared vocabulary for developers to communicate complex ideas and serve as blueprints for building robust applications. These well-defined solutions help overcome the challenges of building large-scale, resilient, and high-performance applications. In the context of serverless computing, these patterns transcend their conventional role, becoming indispensable tools for navigating the peculiar challenges posed by serverless architectures. From managing state in stateless environments to orchestrating microservices and ensuring scalability, design patterns serve as the compass guiding developers through the serverless wilderness.

The journey through serverless architecture patterns is both a theoretical exploration and a practical guide. We'll explore essential patterns such as Function Chaining, Event-Driven Microservices, Fan-Out, API Gateway, and the Aggregator Pattern. Each pattern will be unpacked to reveal its core principles, benefits, and real-world applications, highlighting how they address specific serverless design challenges. Moreover, we will not only discuss these patterns in the abstract but also ground them in practical reality. Through illustrative examples and case studies, you will see these patterns come to life, demonstrating their implementation and impact in real serverless projects.

As we venture into the heart of serverless architecture patterns, remember that the goal is not merely to acquaint you with these patterns but to empower you to apply them confidently in your serverless endeavors. Whether you are designing a new serverless application from the ground up or optimizing an existing project, the insights gained from this chapter will serve as a valuable resource, guiding you towards creating more efficient, scalable, and resilient serverless architectures.

3.2 Why Design Patterns Matter

To design scalable, maintainable, and efficient serverless applications, we must adopt structured design approaches. This is where design patterns play a crucial role. Serverless computing brings an exciting shift in how we build applications, offering unparalleled scalability, cost efficiency, and a strong focus on developer productivity. However, as we embrace serverless paradigms, it's essential to be aware of the unique architectural challenges they present. Distributing application logic across smaller functions, orchestrating asynchronous interactions, and maintaining visibility in complex systems require careful planning and structured approaches.

This is where design patterns come to the forefront. In traditional software development, design patterns have served as blueprints for solving recurring problems, promoting maintainability, and establishing best practices. In the serverless realm, their importance is amplified. Proven patterns offer guidance on structuring our serverless functions, handling events effectively, and building applications that are robust, scalable, and adaptable to evolving business needs.

3.2.1 Addressing Common Serverless Challenges

Serverless computing, for all its advantages, introduces a set of challenges that developers must navigate. These challenges include:

- **Scalability**: While serverless functions inherently scale on demand, architecting an entire application to efficiently handle this scaling requires careful planning and design.

- **Decoupling**: The distributed nature of serverless applications necessitates a high degree of decoupling between components, which can complicate communication and data sharing.

- **Asynchronous Interactions**: Serverless architectures often rely on asynchronous operations, which can introduce complexity in handling and coordinating these interactions.

- **Maintainability**: The granular, function-level deployment of serverless applications can lead to difficulties in managing and maintaining the application as a whole, especially as it grows.

3.2.2 The Role of Design Patterns

In serverless architecture, design patterns serve as a roadmap for making architectural decisions that lead to scalable and efficient applications. They distill the collective experience and wisdom of the software engineering community into actionable strategies, helping developers avoid common pitfalls and accelerate the development process.

By understanding and applying these patterns, developers can more effectively leverage the benefits of serverless computing. Patterns not only offer solutions to technical challenges but also promote best practices that lead to the development of high-quality, scalable, and maintainable serverless applications.

Design patterns in serverless computing serve multiple purposes:

- **Efficiency**: They provide proven strategies for maximizing the efficiency of serverless applications, ensuring resources are used optimally, and that the application scales gracefully.

- **Resilience**: Patterns help in building resilient architectures that can tolerate failures and ensure high availability, which is crucial for mission-critical applications.

- **Simplicity**: By applying well-understood patterns, developers can simplify the complexity inherent in serverless applications, making them easier to build, understand, and maintain.

- **Adaptability**: They allow for the flexible composition of serverless components, facilitating easier changes and additions over the application's lifecycle.

3.3   Key Serverless Patterns

In the previous chapter, we introduced the challenge of building a scalable and responsive e-commerce backend. Now, let's dive into the core serverless patterns that will form the building blocks of our solution. As we explore each pattern, we'll see how it directly addresses the complexities of handling orders, managing inventory, and delivering a seamless user experience.

As we progress, we'll introduce essential serverless patterns and demonstrate how Knative seamlessly integrates these concepts into your development workflow. This exploration will equip you with a comprehensive understanding of serverless patterns within Knative, ensuring you have the knowledge and tools to tackle the unique challenges of building serverless solutions. Through this narrative, the aim is to provide a practical framework for understanding how serverless patterns can be effectively applied in real-world scenarios. By focusing on a tangible example such as an e-commerce backend, the abstract concepts of serverless computing and Knative become grounded, allowing for a deeper comprehension of their benefits and applications. By the end of this chapter, you'll have a better understanding of how to design a resilient, cost-effective, and endlessly adaptable serverless system.

3.4 The Heartbeat: Event-Driven Design

Picture this: a customer clicks the "Buy Now" button on your online storefront. Behind the scenes, a cascade of actions needs to occur — inventory updates, payment processing, delivery management, customer notifications, and many more — all in a timely and reliable manner. Traditional approaches often involve tightly coupling these steps, leading to scalability and maintenance challenges. Serverless event-driven architectures provide a compelling solution to these problems by decoupling components through the use of events.

3.4.1 The Power of Events

The event-driven pattern is an architectural style where components of the application are triggered and communicate via events. These events can be anything from user actions, system states changes, to notifications from other services. In serverless architectures, this pattern is particularly powerful, as it aligns with the on-demand, ephemeral nature of serverless functions, which execute in response to events and scale automatically.

In an event-driven system, individual components react to specific events rather than being directly invoked by other functions. Each step in our order processing flow can be encapsulated in an independent serverless function. When the customer clicks 'Place Order,' an EVENT_ORDER_CREATED event triggers the initial function. Subsequent functions then respond to events emitted throughout the process. Figure 3.1 illustrates the sequence of steps involved in this event-driven process. The event-driven pattern offers several advantages:

- **Decoupling**: Event-driven design allows serverless functions to react to events rather than being directly invoked. This reduces dependencies and tight coupling between components which leads to easier maintenance and scalability.

- **Responsiveness**: Event-driven design allows systems to react to real-time inputs promptly, enhancing user experience and system efficiency.

- **Scalability**: Event-driven design allows serverless functions to automatically scale up or down based on the volume of events. You avoid over-provisioning resources or having bottlenecks during traffic surges.

- **Resilience**: Event-driven systems are inherently more resilient, as functions can react independently to failures, reducing cascading errors.

- **Flexibility**: Event-driven design enables easy integration with external systems and services. New functionality can be added as independent functions that listen for specific events without modifying existing workflows.

- **Developer Agility**: Event-driven design enables functions to focus on specific tasks, making development and updates easier.

- **Cost-efficiency**: In serverless environments, functions run only in response to events, optimizing resource usage and costs since you pay only for the compute resources you use.

While powerful, the event-driven design pattern has key nuances to be considered:

- **Event Management Complexity**: Ensuring the reliable delivery, ordering, and processing of events can introduce complexity, especially in large-scale systems with numerous event sources and targets.

- **Observability**: Monitoring can be more complex as you need to trace events across distributed functions.

- **Debugging**: Debugging event flows and understanding the root cause of issues can require specialized tools.

- **Eventual Consistency**: It's important to design your system with the understanding that there might be delays in how events propagate and designing your application logic to handle them gracefully.

3.4.2 Implementing Event-Driven Pattern

Let's see a simplified example of what happens in our e-commerce system when a user clicks on the Buy Now button. 3.1 represents the sequence diagram of the event-driven process. Our serverless eCommerce application is composed of functions. Each function is independent and reacts to events. Each function also triggers events based on program flow.

The sequence of steps in the sequence diagram are as follows

- User Interaction: User clicks on the "Buy Now button on our e-commerce website.

- Event Generation: The website, acting as a Knative **Event Source** (e.g., an HTTPSource), generates an EVENT_ORDER_CREATED event containing order details.

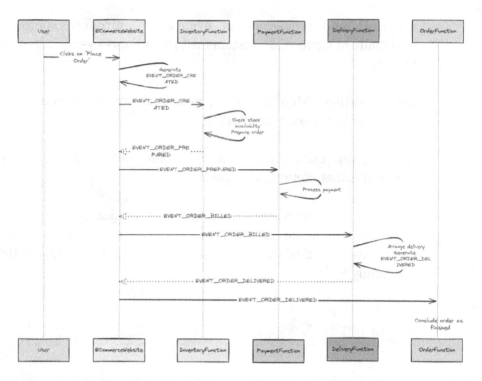

Figure 3.1: Event-Driven Design.

- Event Routing: Knative Eventing routes the event through a **Channel** and **Broker** to ensure reliable delivery to the appropriate subscribers.

- Inventory Function: A Knative **Trigger** filters for EVENT_ORDER_CREATED and activates the InventoryFunction. This function checks stock availability, prepares the order, and emits an EVENT_ORDER_PREPARED event.

- Payment Function: Another **Trigger** listens for EVENT_ORDER_PREPARED and calls the PaymentFunction. This function processes the payment and emits an EVENT_ORDER_BILLED event.

- Delivery Function: A **Trigger** for EVENT_ORDER_BILLED activates the

DeliveryFunction, which arranges product delivery and emits an EVENT_ORDER_DELIVERED event.

- Order Function: Finally, the EVENT_ORDER_DELIVERED event triggers the OrderFunction, which finalizes the order status.

- Error Handling: If any of the above functions fail, the corresponding error events EVENT_INVENTORY_UNAVAILABLE, EVENT_PAYMENT_FAILED, EVENT_DELIVERY_FAILED events are emitted.

The below pseudo-code snippets show the various functions which are triggered by the respective events. These functions also raise events based on program logic. Listing 3.1 demonstrates the initial EVENT_ORDER_CREATED event triggered by the checkout process of the e-commerce website.

```
1   // Define event types (using CloudEvents convention)
2   EVENT_ORDER_CREATED = dev.ecommerce.order.placed
3   EVENT_ORDER_PREPARED = dev.ecommerce.order.prepared
4   EVENT_ORDER_BILLED = dev.ecommerce.order.billed
5   EVENT_ORDER_DELIVERED = dev.ecommerce.order.delivered
6
7   // Error event types
8   EVENT_INVENTORY_UNAVAILABLE =
        dev.ecommerce.order.inventory_unavailable
9   EVENT_PAYMENT_FAILED = dev.ecommerce.order.payment_failed
10  EVENT_DELIVERY_FAILED = dev.ecommerce.order.delivery_failed
11
12  // Event publisher function
13  FUNCTION publishEvent(eventType, eventData)
14      // Publish CloudEvent to the appropriate Knative
        Channel (e.g., KafkaChannel)
15      // Knative aims to provide reliable delivery, often
        with at-least-once semantics
16      // Using Knative Channels like KafkaChannel ensures
        reliable, at-least-once delivery
```

```
17  ENDFUNCTION
18
19
20  // User interaction triggers the order creation event
        (e-commerce website)
21  FUNCTION click_PlaceOrder()
22      orderDetails = GET_ORDER_DETAILS()
23      publishEvent(EVENT_ORDER_CREATED, orderDetails)
24  ENDFUNCTION
```

Listing 3.1: e-Commerce Website Order-Created trigger

The first step is to define the CloudEvent types that will be used throughout the workflow. These events follow the CloudEvents naming convention, which ensures compatibility and makes the system more interoperable with other CloudEvents-based systems. We will explore CloudEvents in more detail in Chapter 8. The publishEvent function is a generic utility function that takes care of publishing CloudEvents to the appropriate Knative channels. It abstracts the complexity of event delivery, ensuring that events are reliably delivered to the subscribers.

The click_PlaceOrder function is executed by the action of a user clicking the "Place Order" button on the e-commerce website. It retrieves the necessary order details (e.g., from a form submission) and then publishes an EVENT_ORDER_CREATED event, which contains these details. This event is the starting point of the order processing workflow.

In listing 3.2 the inventoryFunction is triggered by the EVENT_ORDER_CREATED event. Knative automatically scales this function based on the incoming event load, ensuring it can handle high volumes of orders. The function first extracts the orderId' from the event data and then retrieves the complete order details. It checks if the required items are in stock. If they are, it reserves the stock, updates the inventory, and then publishes an EVENT_ORDER_PREPARED event to trigger the next

step in the workflow. If the items are not available, it publishes an
EVENT_INVENTORY_UNAVAILABLE event to trigger an appropriate error
handling process.

```
1  FUNCTION inventoryFunction(orderCreatedEvent)
2      // Knative automatically scales this function based on
       event load
3      orderId = orderCreatedEvent.data.orderId
4      orderDetails = GET_ORDER_DETAILS(orderId)
5      IF isStockAvailable(orderDetails) THEN
6          // Reserve stock, update inventory, etc.
7          publishEvent(EVENT_ORDER_PREPARED, { orderId:
       orderId,... })
8      ELSE
9          // Handle out-of-stock scenario, publish error event
10         publishEvent(EVENT_INVENTORY_UNAVAILABLE, {
       orderId: orderId,... })
11     ENDIF
12 ENDFUNCTION
```

Listing 3.2: Inventory Function

In listing 3.3 the paymentFunction is triggered by the EVENT_ORDER_PREPARED
event, ensuring it's only called when the order is ready for payment.
Knative's filtering mechanism ensures this function is not invoked
unnecessarily. The function retrieves the payment information
associated with the order and processes the payment. If the payment is
successful, it publishes an EVENT_ORDER_BILLED event. If the payment
fails, it publishes an EVENT_PAYMENT_FAILED event.

```
1  // Payment Function (triggered by Knative Trigger for
       EVENT_ORDER_PREPARED)
2  FUNCTION paymentFunction(orderPreparedEvent)
3      // Knative ensures this function is only invoked for
       relevant events
4      orderId = orderPreparedEvent.data.orderId
```

```
5       paymentInfo = GET_PAYMENT_INFO(orderId)
6
7       IF processPayment(paymentInfo) THEN
8           publishEvent(EVENT_ORDER_BILLED, { orderId:
        orderId,... })
9       ELSE
10          // Handle payment failure, publish error event
11          publishEvent(EVENT_PAYMENT_FAILED, { orderId:
        orderId,... })
12      ENDIF
13  ENDFUNCTION
```

Listing 3.3: Payment Function

In listing 3.4 the deliveryFunction is triggered by the EVENT_ORDER_BILLED event. This ensures the delivery process starts only after successful payment. Knative's loose coupling allows this function to scale independently to handle varying workloads of delivery arrangements. The function retrieves the orderId from the event data and uses it to fetch the customer's shippingAddress from the database. The arrangeDelivery function (not detailed here) encapsulates the logic for coordinating with a shipping provider to schedule the delivery.

```
1   // Delivery Function (triggered by Knative Trigger for
        EVENT_ORDER_BILLED)
2   FUNCTION deliveryFunction(orderBilledEvent)
3       // Knative's loose coupling allows independent scaling
        of this function
4       orderId = orderBilledEvent.data.orderId
5       shippingAddress = GET_SHIPPING_ADDRESS(orderId)
6
7       IF arrangeDelivery(orderId, shippingAddress) THEN
8           publishEvent(EVENT_ORDER_DELIVERED, { orderId:
        orderId,... })
9           publishEvent(EVENT_ORDER_DELIVERED, { orderId:
        orderId,... })
10      ELSE
```

```
11      // Handle delivery failure, publish error event
12          publishEvent(EVENT_DELIVERY_FAILED, { orderId:
        orderId,... })
13      ENDIF
14  ENDFUNCTION
```

Listing 3.4: Delivery Function

The function in listing 3.5 represents the final stage of the order processing workflow. It is triggered by a Knative Trigger that listens for the EVENT_ORDER_DELIVERED event, indicating that the delivery arrangements have been successfully completed. The function extracts the orderId' from the event data and uses it to update the order status in the database to completed' or a similar final state, signifying that the entire order processing cycle is finished.

```
1  // Order Function (triggered by Knative Trigger for
       EVENT_ORDER_DELIVERED)
2  FUNCTION orderFunction(orderDeliveredEvent)
3      orderId = orderDeliveredEvent.data.orderId
4      // Finalize order status in database
5      completeOrder(orderId)
6  ENDFUNCTION
```

Listing 3.5: Order Function

In a robust event-driven system, handling errors gracefully is as important as defining the successful workflow. While the previous code listings demonstrated the happy path of order processing, real-world applications must also account for failures. Error events, such as EVENT_INVENTORY_UNAVAILABLE, EVENT_PAYMENT_FAILED, and EVENT_DELIVERY_FAILED, are crucial for signaling when something goes wrong in the workflow.

Listing 3.6 shows an example of an error handling function, specifically designed to react to the EVENT_PAYMENT_FAILED event. This function demonstrates basic error handling actions such as logging and notification. In a production system, error handling functions would likely include more sophisticated recovery mechanisms, such as retry logic, escalation procedures, or automated notifications to support teams.

```
1   // Error Handler Function (triggered by Knative Trigger for
        EVENT_PAYMENT_FAILED)
2   FUNCTION
        errorHandlerFunction_PaymentFailed(paymentFailedEvent)
3       // This function handles errors specifically related to
        payment failures
4       orderId = paymentFailedEvent.data.orderId
5       paymentErrorDetails =
        paymentFailedEvent.data.errorDetails  // Assume error
        details are in the event data
6
7       // 1. Log the Error for monitoring and debugging
8       LOG_ERROR("Payment processing failed for Order ID: " +
        orderId)
9       LOG_ERROR("Error Details: " + paymentErrorDetails)
10      LOG_ERROR("Event Type: EVENT_PAYMENT_FAILED")
11      LOG_ERROR("Timestamp: " + GET_CURRENT_TIMESTAMP())
12
13      // 2. Send a Notification to Customer Service (or Admin)
14      notificationMessage = "Payment failed for Order ID: " +
        orderId + ". Customer service intervention may be
        required."
15
        SEND_NOTIFICATION_TO_CUSTOMER_SERVICE(notificationMessage)
        // Assume a function to send notifications
16
17      // [Optional:  More advanced error handling could
        include:]
18      // - Implement retry logic (for transient payment
        failures)
```

```
19      // - Publish a "customer_notification_needed" event to
        trigger customer communication
20      // - Update order status to "payment_failed" in the
        database (if not already done)
21
22  ENDFUNCTION
```

Listing 3.6: Error Handler Function (Payment Failed Example)

The errorHandlerFunction_PaymentFailed function, triggered by the EVENT_PAYMENT_FAILED event, exemplifies a basic error handling strategy. It performs two key actions: it logs the error details for system monitoring and debugging, and it sends a notification to customer service, enabling them to take further action. In a more sophisticated system, this error handler could also implement retry logic for transient errors, publish new events to initiate compensatory transactions (like reversing a stock reservation), or update the order status to reflect the payment failure.

This explicit example of an error handler function highlights that in event-driven architectures, error handling is not an afterthought, but an integral part of the design. By defining and implementing functions to react to error events, you can build more resilient and manageable serverless applications. Knative Eventing provides mechanisms for reliable event delivery, which is crucial for ensuring that error events, just like success events, are reliably routed to the appropriate error handling functions.

We have now completed the entire workflow from order creation to order delivery in an event-driven, decoupled, independently scalable and resilient design. This is enabled by the powerful intrinsic mechanisms provided by Knative.

The event-driven pattern is central to leveraging the full potential of serverless computing, offering a model that promotes scalability, flexibility, and cost efficiency. While challenges like event management and system observability persist, the advantages, especially in dynamic and scalable environments like e-commerce, are compelling. Understanding and implementing this pattern effectively paves the way for building responsive, efficient, and modern applications that can adapt to changing demands with ease.

3.4.3 Knative Eventing: Simplifying EDA

Knative Eventing is a core component of Knative that simplifies the development and management of event-driven architectures on Kubernetes. It provides a set of powerful primitives and abstractions that make it easier to build, deploy, and scale event-driven applications. Here's how Knative Eventing facilitates the implementation of the event-driven pattern:

- **Event Sources:** Knative Eventing supports a wide range of event sources, allowing you to connect your serverless functions to various event producers. These sources can include cloud services (e.g., AWS S3, Google Cloud Storage), message brokers (e.g., Apache Kafka, RabbitMQ), and even custom sources that you define yourself. In the e-commerce example, the event source would be triggered when the user clicks "Place Order" on the website.

- **Channels and Brokers:** Knative Channels provide a standardized way to represent a stream of events. Knative Brokers act as intermediaries, routing events from sources to the appropriate consumers based on event attributes and subscription rules. This allows for events like EVENT_ORDER_CREATED to be reliably delivered to the appropriate functions.

- **Triggers and Subscriptions:** Knative Triggers define the relationship between an event source and the serverless functions that should respond to it. You can configure triggers to filter events based on specific criteria, ensuring that functions only receive the events they are interested in. In our example, triggers ensure that the InventoryFunction is only called when an EVENT_ORDER_CREATED event occurs. Subscriptions link channels to triggers, enabling the flow of events through your system, as depicted in Figure 3.1.

- **Triggers and Subscriptions:** Knative Triggers define the relationship between an event source and the serverless functions that should respond to it. You can configure triggers to filter events based on specific criteria, ensuring that functions only receive the events they are interested in. In our example, triggers ensure that the InventoryFunction is only called when an EVENT_ORDER_CREATED event occurs. Subscriptions link channels to triggers, enabling the flow of events through your system, as depicted in Figure 3.1.

3.4.4 Event-Driven Design: Knative Benefits

- **Loose Coupling:** Services react to events, not direct calls, promoting independent development and scaling. This is evident in the diagram where each function operates independently after receiving the relevant event.

- **Scalability:** Knative automatically scales functions based on event volume, ensuring responsiveness under load. This is crucial for e-commerce platforms where traffic can vary significantly.

- **Resilience:** Event-driven systems can handle failures gracefully, as functions operate independently. If the PaymentFunction fails, it doesn't necessarily block the DeliveryFunction from processing successful orders.

- **Flexibility:** New functions can be added to react to events without disrupting existing workflows. In our example, you could add a `Fraud Detection Function` triggered by `EVENT_ORDER_CREATED` without modifying the existing flow.

By leveraging Knative Eventing, you can build event-driven serverless applications that are scalable, resilient, and adaptable to changing requirements. Whether you're building an e-commerce platform, a real-time data processing pipeline, or any other event-driven system, Knative provides the tools and abstractions to simplify your development and accelerate your innovation.

3.5   Function Chaining Design Pattern

Function chaining involves linking together multiple serverless functions in a specific sequence, where the output of one function serves as the input to the next. This creates a chain of operations that can execute complex, multi-step processes in an orderly manner. Orchestration extends this concept by managing these chains, including error handling, branching, and state management, to coordinate more complex workflows. Function chaining, and more sophisticated patterns like sagas, provide the tools to manage these complex workflows.

In function chaining design pattern, the output of one serverless function becomes the input to the next, creating a well-defined process. For e.g, In our e-commerce system, processes like discounting often involve multiple steps that must occur in a specific sequence. Figure 3.2 illustrates how we could implement a personalized discount generation process using function chaining. Function chaining and orchestration provide the tools to manage these workflows.

The function chaining pattern provides the following benefits

- **Modularity**: Breaks down complex processes into smaller, manageable, reusable functions.

- **Flexibility**: Chains can be easily reconfigured or extended as workflows evolve.

- **Error Handling**: Orchestration allows for sophisticated error management strategies, ensuring the entire workflow can gracefully handle and recover from failures at any step.

- **Scalability**: Each function in the chain can scale independently, allowing the system to efficiently handle varying loads.

- **Cost Optimization**: Functions execute only when triggered by the output of the preceding function, aligning resource usage closely with actual needs and minimizing idle time.

- **Simplified Development**: Developers can focus on the logic of individual steps without being bogged down by the complexities of the entire workflow.

While powerful, function chaining pattern has nuances to consider:

- **Complex Workflow Management**: As chains grow in complexity, orchestrating these workflows and maintaining state between functions become challenging.

- **Latency**: Each function call introduces network latency, which can accumulate across a long chain, impacting performance.

- **Error Propagation**: Errors in early steps can propagate through the chain, requiring comprehensive error handling strategies.

While these challenges are important to consider, the improvements in modularity, maintainability, and scalability provided by function chaining often outweigh the challenges in real-world serverless applications.

3.5.1 Implementing Function Chaining pattern

In our e-commerce platform, enhancing customer satisfaction and incentivizing purchases are crucial. A personalized discount generation process, triggered when a customer proceeds to checkout, can significantly improve the shopping experience and lead to higher order rates. This process involves analyzing the customer's shopping history, current cart items, and their loyalty tier to generate a tailored discount code to be applied at checkout. Figure 3.2 illustrates how we could implement this personalized discount generation process using function chaining

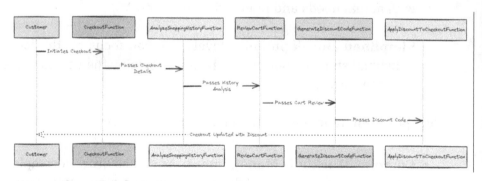

Figure 3.2: Function Chaining Pattern

The sequence of steps in the checkout process are as follows

- Checkout: CheckoutFunction is triggered first by the customer's action to initiate checkout. This function prepares the necessary data (e.g., customer ID, cart contents) and calls the next function in the sequence.

- Analyze Shopping History: AnalyzeShoppingHistoryFunction is called next with data passed from the previous function. It analyzes the customers shopping history to determine eligibility for certain discounts or promotions, then passes its findings to the next function.

- Review Cart: The ReviewCartFunction receives the output from AnalyzeShoppingHistoryFunction along with the original checkout data. It performs further analysis, such as checking for additional discounts applicable based on the current cart contents, then calls the next function with its compiled data.

- Generate Discount: GenerateDiscountCodeFunction is triggered by ReviewCartFunction and uses all the accumulated data to generate a personalized discount code. Once the discount code is generated, it passes this information along to the final function in the chain.

- Apply Discount: ApplyDiscountToCheckoutFunction is the last function in the sequence. It applies the discount code to the customer's total purchase amount, and optionally confirms the successful application of the discount to the customer.

The below pseudo-code snippets demonstrate an implementation of function chaining to implement the discount coupon generation workflow.

The checkoutFunction' function in listing 3.7 initiates the discount generation process. It receives an event (e.g., from a Proceed to Checkout' button click) containing customerID' and cartDetails. It then calls the analyzeShoppingHistoryFunction' in listing 3.8, passing the relevant data as input.

```
1    FUNCTION checkoutFunction(event)
```

```
2      // Assume event contains customerID and cartDetails
3      customerID = event.customerID
4      cartDetails = event.cartDetails
5
6      // Call the next function in the chain with
       necessary details
7          analyzeShoppingHistoryFunction({customerID,
       cartDetails})
8      ENDFUNCTION
```

Listing 3.7: Checkout Function

The analyzeShoppingHistoryFunction function in listing 3.8 analyzes the customer's shopping history to determine their eligibility for discounts. It receives customerID, cartDetails, and potentially other relevant data from the previous function. The analysis could involve calculating the customer's total spending, frequency of purchases, etc. The result of this analysis is then passed, along with the original input data, to the reviewCartFunction in listing 3.9.

```
1   FUNCTION analyzeShoppingHistoryFunction(input)
2       {customerID, cartDetails} = input
3
4       // Perform analysis on customer's shopping history
5       // (e.g., calculate total spending, frequency of
        purchases)
6
7       analysisResult = ANALYZE_SHOPPING_HISTORY(customerID)
8
9       // Pass the analysis result and original input to the
        next function
10      reviewCartFunction({customerID, cartDetails,
        analysisResult})
11  ENDFUNCTION
```

Listing 3.8: AnalyzeShoppingHistory Function

The reviewCartFunction function in listing 3.9 takes the analysisResult from the previous function and the current cartDetails to determine the best possible discount for the customer. It might consider factors like the customer's loyalty tier, eligible products in the cart, and any ongoing promotions. The outcome of this review is then passed to the generateDiscountCodeFunction in listing 3.10.

```
1   FUNCTION reviewCartFunction(input)
2       {customerID, cartDetails, analysisResult} = input
3
4       // Review the current cart in the context of the
        analysis result
5       // (e.g., check for eligible products, apply tier-based
        discounts)
6
7       cartReviewResult = REVIEW_CART(cartDetails,
        analysisResult)
8
9       // Generate a discount code based on the cart review
        and analysis
10      generateDiscountCodeFunction({customerID,
        cartReviewResult})
11  ENDFUNCTION
```

Listing 3.9: ReviewCart Function

The function in listing 3.10 creates a unique discount code based on the cartReviewResult. The logic here could be complex, considering various factors and business rules to determine the most appropriate discount percentage or amount. The generated discountCode' is passed to the final function in the chain.

```
1   FUNCTION generateDiscountCodeFunction(input)
2       {customerID, cartReviewResult} = input
3
```

```
4     // Logic to generate a personalized discount code based
      on the review results
5
6     discountCode = GENERATE_DISCOUNT_CODE(cartReviewResult)
7
8     // Apply the discount code to the checkout process
9     applyDiscountToCheckoutFunction({customerID,
      discountCode})
10  ENDFUNCTION
```

Listing 3.10: GenerateDiscountCode Function

The last function in the chain in listing 3.11 applies the 'discountCode' to the customer's order, updating the total cost accordingly. It could also optionally emit an event (e.g., EVENT_DISCOUNT_APPLIED') to trigger further actions like sending a confirmation email to the customer. Once the discount is applied, the checkout process is considered complete, and the order can proceed to the next stages like billing and delivery.

```
1   FUNCTION applyDiscountToCheckoutFunction(input)
2       {customerID, discountCode} = input
3
4       // Apply the discount code to the customer's checkout
5       APPLY_DISCOUNT(customerID, discountCode)
6
7       // Optionally, emit an event to indicate the discount
        has been applied
8       publishEvent(EVENT_DISCOUNT_APPLIED, {customerID,
        discountCode})
9
10      // Checkout process is completed, and the order
        proceeds to billing/delivery
11  ENDFUNCTION
```

Listing 3.11: ApplyDiscountToCheckout Function

In the above pseudo-code the output of each function forms the input to the next function in the chain. The `AnalyzeShoppingHistory` function outputs shopping history details for the customer, which then forms the input to the `ReviewCartFunction`. The chain extends with the output of each function forming the input to the next function. Each function performs a specific action that is decoupled and independent of all other functionality.

3.6 The Doorway: API Gateway Pattern

Ever struggled to make backend changes without breaking your application? Wish you could update the product search functionality in your eCommerce application without risking the checkout process? That's where the API Gateway pattern comes to the rescue. So, how does the API Gateway pattern solve this problem? Imagine your e-commerce backend is a bustling marketplace with multiple stores(functions). The API Gateway is the friendly gatekeeper, making sure every customer (request) gets to the right place.

The API Gateway pattern plays a pivotal role in modern serverless architectures, offering a unified interface to a collection of serverless functions. It acts as an orchestration layer that directs client requests to the appropriate backend function based on different criteria.

The API Gateway handles cross-cutting concerns such as authentication, rate limiting, CORS (Cross-Origin Resource Sharing) policies, SSL termination among others. Cross-cutting concerns are aspects of a system that affect multiple components and are best handled centrally rather than repeated across various functions. It streamlines interactions between clients and services, bolsters security, enhances performance, and simplifies operational processes in serverless architectures. This centralized approach not only elevates the developer and user experience but also contributes to a more robust, efficient, and cost-effective system.

Utilizing the API Gateway as a caching layer is a powerful strategy to enhance the performance, scalability, and cost-effectiveness of serverless architectures. Caching enhances the system's ability to handle spikes in traffic by offloading requests from the backend services. This is particularly crucial in serverless architectures, where the ability to scale rapidly in response to demand is a key advantage.

The API Gateway pattern offers numerous advantages when implemented within a serverless architecture:

- **Simplified Client Interaction**: Clients interact with a single, well-defined API surface exposed by the gateway, shielding them from the intricacies of how various serverless functions interact on the backend. It's an architectural element that allows for efficient, secure, and manageable interactions between clients and serverless functions. This allows for cleaner and more maintainable client-side code. For instance, a mobile app can leverage the `/products` endpoint for querying product information without needing to know the specifics of how the product data is retrieved and transformed from multiple backend services.

- **Decoupling**: Clients interact with the API Gateway, not directly with backend services. This promotes loose coupling between the frontend and backend, enabling independent development and deployment cycles for each. Frontend teams can update the client-side logic without needing changes to the backend services and vice versa.

- **Enhanced Security**: Centralizing authentication and authorization at the API Gateway strengthens the overall security posture. Common security tasks like SSL termination, user authentication (e.g. JWT validation), and authorization checks (enforcing access control to sensitive order data) can be implemented effectively at this layer. In an e-commerce application, the API Gateway can ensure only authorized users can access the `/customer/orders` endpoint and prevent unauthorized attempts to modify order details.

- **Performance Optimization**: The API Gateway can be configured to improve client experience through techniques like response caching, request batching, and content negotiation. Caching frequently accessed data at the API Gateway reduces the load on backend services and improves response times for clients.

- **Cost-Effectiveness**: By reducing the number of direct calls to backend services and potentially leveraging caching mechanisms, the API Gateway can contribute to minimizing the overall cost of serverless function execution. Serverless functions are typically billed per execution, so optimizing request handling at the gateway can lead to significant cost savings.

- **Monitoring and Management**: The API Gateway acts as a central point for logging, tracing, and monitoring API usage and performance. This observability allows for proactive identification and resolution of issues, ensuring a smooth user experience for your system.

While the API Gateway pattern offers undeniable advantages, it's essential to acknowledge the potential challenges:

- **Complexity & Overhead**: Configuring and managing an API Gateway introduces additional complexity compared to a simpler architecture where clients directly invoke backend functions. However, the benefits often outweigh this overhead in terms of maintainability, security, and scalability.

- **Vendor Lock-in**: Cloud providers often offer managed API Gateway solutions. While convenient, these can introduce vendor lock-in, making it more difficult to migrate to a different platform in the future.

- **Consistency Across Environments**: Ensuring the API Gateway behaves consistently across development, testing, and production environments can be challenging. Careful configuration management and infrastructure-as-code practices are essential.

By default, Knative uses Istio as its ingress gateway manager. Knative can be used in conjunction with Ambassador or Kong as an API Gateway. This allows us to leverage the ability to efficiently route external traffic to Knative services, benefiting from the simplicity of these cloud native API gateways and Knative's serverless capabilities. These API gateways offer a streamlined approach to managing ingress traffic with features such as automatic HTTPS, load balancing, support for gRPC, WebSockets, and HTTP/2. They can also be used to manage security aspects such as API key management, OAuth 2.0, JWT authentication, and CORS policies, providing a secure gateway for accessing your Knative services.

3.6.1 Implementing API Gateway Pattern

In our e-commerce platform, product listings are frequently requested yet only updated on a daily basis. Leveraging the API Gateway for caching these listings dramatically enhances the user experience. Subsequent requests for product listings can be served directly from the cache, significantly reducing response times and decreasing the load on the backend product listing service.

Imagine a customer browsing your product catalog. With API Gateway caching, popular product listings can be stored directly at the gateway.

When a customer requests the Top 10 Laptops page, it loads instantly, without needing to go to the product database each time. Figure 3.3 illustrates how product listing can be optimized using the API Gateway pattern.

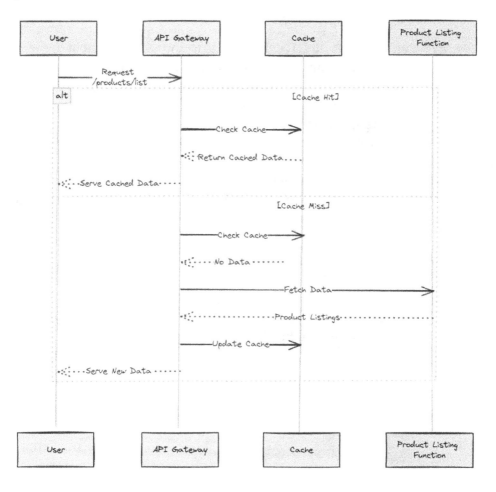

Figure 3.3: API Gateway Pattern

The sequence of steps in listing products is as follows

- The client sends a request to the API Gateway to list products (e.g., /products/list endpoint).

- The API Gateway checks its cache to determine if there's a cached response for the product listing request.

- If a cache hit occurs (cached data is found), the cached response is immediately returned to the client, skipping the backend service interaction.

- If the cache does not contain the requested data (cache miss), the process proceeds to fetch data from the Product Listing function.

- Upon receiving the response from the Product Listing function, the API Gateway updates its cache with the new product listing data to serve future requests more efficiently.

- The API Gateway sends the product listing data back to the client, completing the request cycle.

The below pseudocode snippet in listing 3.12shows how an API Gateway can be used to serve product listing by caching responses.

```
1   function apiGateway(request) {
2
3       // Routing and handling based on request path
4       switch (request.path) {
5           case /products/list:
6               // Integrated Caching Logic
7               if (isCached(request.path)) {
8                   // If response is cached, retrieve from
        cache
9                   return getCachedResponse(request.path);
10              } else {
```

```
11          // If not cached, fetch product list from
        the ProductService
12              let productList = fetchProductList();
13              // Cache the response for future requests
14              cacheResponse(request.path, productList);
15              // Return the fresh product list
16              return productList;
17          }
18          return handleProductListRequest(request);
19      default:
20          return { status: 404 Not Found };
21          return { status: 404 Not Found };
22      }
23  }
```

Listing 3.12: Checkout Function

Another critical aspect of the API Gateway pattern is managing authentication and authorization. In an e-commerce platform, ensuring that only authenticated users access sensitive endpoints is paramount. The API Gateway handles this by implementing crucial tasks like user authentication, authorization, and routing requests to the appropriate backend services. It ensures that cross-cutting concerns like security are managed centrally, enhancing the overall security posture of the system.

Imagine a customer checking their order history. Ensuring secure access to customer-specific information such as order history is paramount. The API Gateway facilitates this by managing user authentication and authorization, ensuring that only authorized requests access sensitive endpoints like `/customer/orders`.

The sequence of steps in listing all orders for a particular customer are as follows.

• The client sends a request to the API Gateway to list orders for a particular customer (e.g., /customer/orders endpoint).

- The API Gateway receives the request and calls the authentication service to verify the identity of the requester.

- If authentication fails, the API Gateway returns an authentication failure response to the client.

- If authentication succeeds, the process moves to the next step.

- The API Gateway calls the authorization service if the authenticated user is authorized to access the /customers/orders endpoint.

- If authorization fails, the process stops, and an `Authorization Failed` response is returned.

- If authorization succeeds, the API Gateway invokes the Order Listing function to fetch the list of orders from the Order Listing function,

- The API Gateway sends the list of orders back to the client, completing the request cycle.

The Figure 3.4 illustrates how the API Gateway pattern can be used to enforce authentication and authorization in an e-commerce platform. Pay close attention to the alternative paths based on the success or failure of authentication and authorization checks. The API Gateway acts as the central point for managing these security aspects, ensuring that only authenticated and authorized users can access sensitive endpoints. These cross-cutting concerns are crucial for securing your serverless architecture and protecting sensitive data. Implementing these checks at the API Gateway level ensures a consistent and robust security posture across your application.

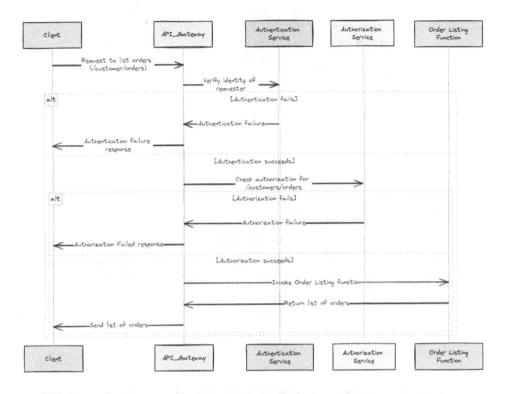

Figure 3.4: API Gateway Pattern

The below pseudocode snippet shows how an API Gateway can be used to centralize authentication & authorization functionality in the API gateway.

```
1  function apiGateway(request) {
2  // Centralized Authentication & Authorization
3  if (!authenticateAndAuthorize(request)) {
4      return { status: Authentication or Authorization
   Failed };
5  }
6
7  // Routing and handling based on request path
```

```
 8      switch (request.path) {
 9          case /customer/orders:
10              let customerOrders =
        fetchCustomerOrders(request.customerId);
11              return customerOrders;
12          default:
13              return { status: 404 Not Found };
14      }
15  }
```

Listing 3.13: Checkout Function

The API Gateway pattern is indispensable in serverless architecture for e-commerce platforms, offering a secure, scalable, and manageable way to expose backend services to clients. While it comes with its set of challenges, the benefits of using an API Gateway, especially in conjunction with serverless functions and Knative, make it a powerful tool in architecting modern, efficient web applications.

3.7 Fan-Out for Parallelism

In serverless architectures, where speed and efficiency are paramount, the Fan-Out pattern emerges as a powerful tool for achieving parallelism and optimizing workflows. This pattern involves broadcasting a single event to multiple recipients simultaneously, enabling them to perform their tasks concurrently.

Imagine an e-commerce platform where a new order triggers a series of independent actions: updating inventory, sending a confirmation email, notifying the warehouse, and updating analytics dashboards. With the Fan-Out pattern, these actions can be executed in parallel, significantly reducing the overall processing time and enhancing the customer experience.

Benefits of Fan-Out:

- **Reduced Latency:** Parallel execution of independent tasks minimizes the overall processing time.

- **Improved Responsiveness:** Faster processing leads to quicker responses for users and improved system efficiency.

- **Increased Throughput:** The ability to handle multiple tasks concurrently increases the system's capacity to process events.

- **Enhanced Scalability:** Each recipient of the event can scale independently based on its workload.

3.7.1 Implementing the Fan-Out Pattern

Imagine an e-commerce platform where a new order triggers a series of independent actions: updating inventory, sending a confirmation email, notifying the warehouse, and updating analytics dashboards. With the Fan-Out pattern, these actions can be executed in parallel, significantly reducing the overall processing time and enhancing the customer experience. Figure 3.5 illustrates how a new order can trigger parallel actions using the Fan-Out pattern.

The sequence of steps involved in processing a new order using the Fan-Out pattern is as follows:

- A customer places a new order on the e-commerce website.

- The website sends an order creation event to a message broker (e.g., Knative Channel).

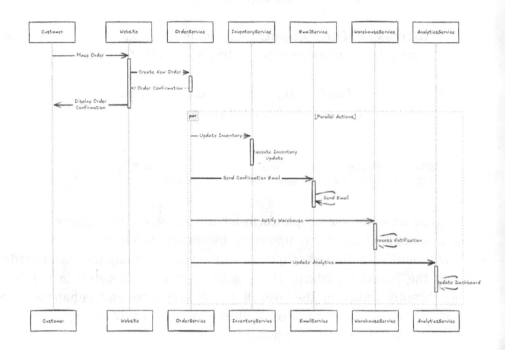

Figure 3.5: Fan-Out Pattern

- The message broker distributes the event to multiple subscribers: Inventory service, Email service, Warehouse service, and Analytics service.

- Each subscriber performs its task independently and concurrently:

  - The Inventory service updates the inventory.

  - The Email service sends an order confirmation email to the customer.

  - The Warehouse service receives a notification for order fulfillment.

  - The Analytics service updates the analytics dashboard with the new order data.

- Once all subscribers have processed the event, the order processing is complete.

The pseudocode snippet below demonstrates how a message broker can be used to distribute an order event to multiple subscribers.

```
1  FUNCTION handleOrderEvent(orderEvent)
2      // Publish the order event to the message broker
3      PUBLISH_EVENT(orderEvent, "order_events_channel")
4  ENDFUNCTION
```

Listing 3.14: Order Event Distribution

3.8   Aggregator Pattern for Insights

The Aggregator pattern plays a crucial role in serverless architectures when you need to gather and process data from multiple sources to gain insights or make informed decisions. This pattern involves a central aggregator component that collects data from various sources, consolidates it, and provides a unified view.

Our e-commerce platform needs to provide personalized product recommendations. The aggregator would gather data from various sources, such as the customer's order history, browsing behavior, product reviews, and social media activity. The real power of the aggregator pattern lies in its ability to optimize data fetching and processing through parallelism, caching, and event-driven mechanisms. It would then consolidate this data, apply filtering and ranking algorithms, and generate a list of relevant recommendations. Figure 3.6 illustrates how an aggregator can gather data from disparate sources and provide a unified view.

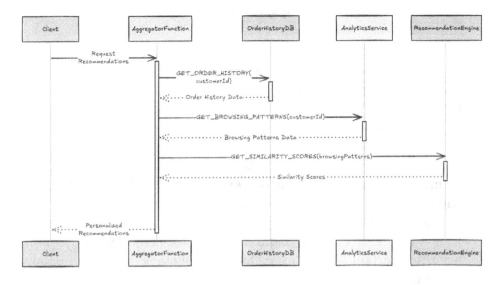

Figure 3.6: Aggregator Pattern

Benefits of Aggregator:

- **Centralized Data Management:** Simplifies workflows by aggregating data into a single point for processing.

- **Improved Data Consistency:** Ensures data consistency by consolidating information from different sources.

- **Enhanced Decision Making:** Facilitates informed decision-making by providing a comprehensive view of the data.

- **Simplified Data Access:** Offers a unified interface for accessing aggregated data.

3.8.1 Implementing the Aggregator Pattern

To enhance the customer experience in our e-commerce system, we want to provide personalized product recommendations. This requires gathering diverse data: order history, browsing patterns, and similarity relationships between products.

The aggregator pattern allows us to encapsulate recommendation logic within a dedicated function or service, making it easier to maintain and update. It enables the seamless collection of results from multiple sources that might have different response times (fetching order history from a database vs. querying a similarity service). The aggregator can prioritize certain data sources, filter out-of-stock items, and potentially cache results for faster retrieval.

The sequence of steps involved in generating product recommendations using the Aggregator pattern is as follows:

- The aggregator function is triggered by an event (e.g., customer login, product page view).

- The aggregator function identifies the relevant data sources based on the triggering event and the customer's context.

- The aggregator function retrieves data from multiple sources concurrently (e.g., order history from the database, browsing patterns from the analytics service, product similarity from a recommendation engine).

- The aggregator function consolidates the data from different sources, applying any necessary transformations or filtering.

- The aggregator function applies ranking or scoring algorithms to prioritize the recommendations based on relevance, popularity, and other factors.

- The aggregator function returns the personalized product recommendations to the client application.

The pseudocode snippet below demonstrates how an aggregator function can gather data from multiple sources and generate product recommendations.

```
FUNCTION generateRecommendations(customerId)
    // Retrieve order history from the database
    orderHistory = GET_ORDER_HISTORY(customerId)

    // Fetch browsing patterns from the analytics service
    browsingPatterns = GET_BROWSING_PATTERNS(customerId)

    // Get product similarity scores from the recommendation
        engine
    similarityScores = GET_SIMILARITY_SCORES(browsingPatterns)

    // Consolidate and filter recommendations based on order
        history, browsing patterns, and similarity scores
    recommendations = AGGREGATE_RECOMMENDATIONS(orderHistory,
        browsingPatterns, similarityScores)

    // Return the personalized product recommendations
    RETURN recommendations
ENDFUNCTION
```

Listing 3.15: Aggregator Function

This approach demonstrates how the aggregator pattern simplifies the integration of multiple data sources, ensures scalability, and delivers a unified view for personalized experiences. By efficiently processing data, the aggregator enables serverless architectures to provide insightful, reliable, and actionable outputs.

3.9 Patterns for Serverless Success

In this chapter, we explored the fundamental building blocks of serverless architecture through a collection of essential design patterns. These patterns — ranging from the **API Gateway** to the **Event-Driven**, **Function Chaining**, **Fan-Out**, and **Aggregator** patterns — highlighted the importance of structured approaches in designing scalable, efficient, and resilient serverless systems.

The chapter demonstrated how these patterns solve specific challenges in serverless architectures:

- **API Gateway Pattern:** Enables centralized routing, authentication, and caching for efficient client-server interactions.

- **Event-Driven Pattern:** Capitalizes on the inherent scalability of serverless functions, creating decoupled, asynchronous workflows.

- **Function Chaining Pattern:** Orchestrates multi-step processes with modularity and flexibility.

- **Fan-Out Pattern:** Unlocks parallelism, reducing latency and increasing throughput by broadcasting events to multiple services.

- **Aggregator Pattern:** Provides a unified view by consolidating data from multiple sources, enabling insightful decision-making.

Each pattern demonstrated how serverless principles, when combined with structured design methodologies, enable scalable and maintainable architectures. By applying these patterns effectively, architects and developers can tackle the complexities of serverless systems while maximizing scalability, maintainability, and responsiveness.

3.9.1 Looking Ahead

As we conclude this exploration of serverless architecture patterns, it is crucial to recognize that no single pattern operates in isolation. Real-world systems often combine these patterns, leveraging their strengths to address complex requirements. For example:

- An **event-driven workflow** may trigger **function chains** for order processing.

- The results of these workflows could be **fanned out** to multiple services for concurrent actions.

- An **API Gateway** might expose these capabilities securely to external users, while an **aggregator** provides unified insights.

In later chapters — particularly Chapter 9 — we will explore the practical implementation of these patterns using Knative Eventing and Serving. We'll revisit these patterns in the context of Knative Eventing, showcasing advanced orchestration, failure handling, and multi-tenant environments.

3.9.2 The Path Forward: Knative Serving

With a solid understanding of serverless architecture patterns, we are now ready to transition from theory to practice. In **Part 2: Building Serverless Applications with Knative Serving**, we will explore how these patterns come to life using **Knative Serving**, a powerful framework for deploying and managing serverless applications on Kubernetes.

The next section will transition from theory to practice through setting up Knative Serving, deploying your first serverless application, and integrating the patterns discussed in this chapter. Together, we will unlock the potential of Knative to build scalable, resilient, and cost-effective serverless solutions.

With these architectural patterns in place, we are now ready to bring our serverless applications to life. Now that we've explored core serverless patterns, let's see how to deploy our first serverless application using Knative Serving in Chapter 4. In the next part, we will dive into Knative Serving and explore how to implement these principles in practice.

Part II

Building Serverless Applications with Knative Serving

4

Knative Serving Essentials

How do you deploy a serverless application on Kubernetes while ensuring it scales seamlessly and remains cost-efficient? What if you could automate scaling, traffic management, and version control with minimal effort? This is where Knative Serving comes in. Welcome to Part 2, where we move from serverless theory to practical implementation. In the previous chapters, we established the fundamentals of serverless computing and explored Knative's role in enabling serverless architectures. Now, it's time to put these concepts into action. This chapter introduces Knative Serving, the component responsible for deploying and managing your serverless workloads on Kubernetes.

The previous chapters have laid the groundwork for our journey into the world of serverless computing with Knative. We've explored the core principles that make serverless architectures so compelling: the ability to scale applications effortlessly, pay only for the resources we actually use, and free developers from the burden of infrastructure management. We've also introduced Knative, the powerful open-source framework that extends Kubernetes to provide a seamless serverless experience. Now, it's time to put these concepts into action. In this chapter, we'll transition from theory to practice, focusing on Knative Serving, the component responsible for deploying and managing your serverless applications on Kubernetes. This chapter provides a comprehensive introduction to Knative Serving's core components and how they work together to simplify the deployment and management of your serverless workloads.

By the end of this chapter, you'll have a solid understanding of:

- Understand the core components of Knative Serving, including Services, Routes, Revisions, and Configurations.
- Learn how these components work together to simplify deployment and traffic management.
- Explore the benefits of using Knative Serving for building and scaling containerized applications.

Through practical examples and clear explanations, we'll guide you through the process of deploying your first serverless application with Knative Serving. You'll learn how to configure scaling parameters, manage traffic between different versions of your application, and ensure that your services are always available and responsive to user demands. By the end of this chapter, you'll have a solid foundation for building and deploying production-ready serverless applications on Kubernetes with Knative Serving. So, let's get started and unleash the power of serverless on your Kubernetes clusters!

4.1 Introduction to Knative Serving

Building upon the serverless architectural patterns detailed in Chapter 3, Knative Serving embodies these concepts through its highly optimized components designed for serverless environments on Kubernetes. This part of the book focuses on translating these abstract principles of serverless architecture into concrete implementations using Knative Serving, which simplifies the management of applications by automating complex Kubernetes operations.

Knative Serving introduces a set of high-level abstractions that streamline the deployment, scaling, and management of serverless applications. By providing these abstractions, Knative Serving allows developers to focus on writing code without needing to manage the underlying infrastructure details. This is crucial for enhancing developer productivity and optimizing operational efficiency.

4.1.1 Core Components of Knative Serving

Before we dive deeper into each component, let's outline the primary building blocks provided by Knative Serving that we will explore in this chapter:

- **Services**: The fundamental unit of deployment in Knative, Services handle the lifecycle management of your applications. They ensure that your serverless functions are deployed, updated, and scaled back down to zero when not in use, all without manual intervention.

- **Routes**: These control the traffic flow to different versions of your applications, enabling strategies such as canary releases and blue/green deployments. Routes in Knative are dynamic, allowing for real-time traffic management that is essential for testing new features and rolling out updates with minimal risk.

- **Revisions**: Each update or modification to a Knative Service creates a new Revision. These are immutable snapshots of your application's configuration and code at a specific point in time. Revisions are crucial for version control and rollbacks, providing a reliable method for managing changes in a serverless environment.

- **Configurations**: These define the desired state of a Service, including its code and runtime settings. Configurations ensure that each version of a Service is reproducible and can be automatically managed by Knative to meet the specified requirements, such as scaling and environmental variables.

4.1.2 Deployment Workflow

To fully leverage Knative Serving, it's important to understand how its components interact during deployment. Knative follows a structured workflow designed to support seamless continuous delivery and agile development. For instance, when a developer pushes changes to a Service, Knative automatically creates a new Revision and updates the Route to gradually shift traffic to the new version, depending on predefined criteria.

This intelligent handling of deployments and traffic routing not only reduces the potential for errors but also aligns with the serverless goal of minimizing operational overhead. The following sections of this chapter will provide a comprehensive exploration of each component, complete with practical examples and best practices to ensure you can apply these concepts effectively in your projects.

4.2 Services: Your Application Foundation

At the core of Knative Serving lies the Service resource, the entry point for your application that efficiently manages its entire lifecycle. Imagine the product listing page on your e-commerce platform. During peak shopping seasons or flash sales, this page experiences a surge in traffic, potentially overwhelming your infrastructure and leading to slowdowns or even crashes. Conversely, during off-peak hours, maintaining a full fleet of servers to handle just a trickle of requests is wasteful and costly.

Knative Services address this challenge head-on. They act as the central unit of management for stateless deployments, providing a higher-level abstraction over raw Kubernetes resources. This abstraction simplifies the complexities of application lifecycle management and empowers you with features like automatic scaling and rollbacks. Think of a Service as a blueprint that declares your application's desired state, encompassing the container image to run, environment variables to configure, and scaling parameters to define how your application responds to demand.

In the context of our e-commerce platform, a Knative Service could encapsulate the logic for handling product listings. During peak traffic, Knative would automatically scale up the number of instances of this service to ensure responsiveness. Conversely, during lulls in activity, it would scale down, potentially even to zero, optimizing resource utilization and minimizing costs. The result is an e-commerce platform that is both highly performant and cost-effective, adapting seamlessly to the ebb and flow of customer traffic.

Let's dig deeper into the essential components of a Knative Service and see how they collaborate to create a smooth serverless experience.

4.2.1 Container Image: The Core of Your App

The container image is where your application's executable code resides. In our e-commerce platform, the product-listing service's code, encompassing the logic to fetch and display product information, would be packaged into a container image. This image, a snapshot of the application's runtime environment, would then be stored in a container registry, ready to be deployed by Knative Serving whenever needed. This setup allows for quick scaling and consistent deployment across various environments.

- **Image Location**: Specify the location of the product listing container image in a registry accessible to your Kubernetes cluster, such as Harbor, Docker Hub, Google Container Registry, or your private registry.

```
1   spec:
2     containers:
3     - image: my-registry/product-listing:v1.2.0
4
```

Listing 4.1: Service definition

- **Versioning is Key**: Utilize image tags to manage versions of your application, enabling controlled deployments and rollbacks. Always prefer specific version tags over mutable tags like latest.

- **Build Automation**: Tools like Cartographer or Tekton can automate the workflow from code repository to container registry, ensuring that every code change triggers the creation of a new, versioned image and corresponding Revision in Knative.

4.2.2 Environment Variables: Runtime Configuration

Environment variables offer a flexible way to inject configuration into your application at runtime. They can be used to configure operational parameters for the product-listing service, such as database connections or feature flags for A/B testing different product display layouts. For example, environment variables might be set to connect to a specific database or toggle new layout features, allowing for dynamic adjustments without needing to alter the application's code. This approach ensures that sensitive information is kept separate from the application code, enhancing security and maintainability.

- **Database Connection Details & Third-Party API Keys**: Use environment variables to pass database URLs and credentials, ideally sourced from Kubernetes Secrets for enhanced security. This also enables you to integrate with external services without redeploying your application.

```
spec:
    containers:
    - image: my-registry/product-listing:v1.2.0
      envFrom:
      - secretRef:
          name: my-database-secret
```

Listing 4.2: Service definition

- **Feature Flags**: Dynamically control feature availability or integrate with external services without redeploying your application.

```
1  spec:
2  containers:
3    - image: my-registry/product-listing:v1.2.0
4      env:
5        - name: FEATURE_X_ENABLED
6          value: true
7
```

Listing 4.3: Service definition

- **Best Practices**: Leverage Kubernetes ConfigMaps and Secrets to manage configuration data and sensitive information outside your application code, reducing risk and promoting separation of concerns.

4.2.3 Scaling Parameters: Your Starting Point

The product-listing service experiences significant traffic fluctuations, with spikes during sales or new product launches. To ensure optimal performance and resource utilization, we can leverage Knative's scaling parameters. By setting the minScale to a value greater than zero, we ensure that at least one instance of the service is always running, eliminating cold start delays even during periods of low activity. The maxScale can be set to a reasonable upper limit to prevent excessive resource consumption during peak traffic. Knative's auto-scaling capabilities begin with your Service's scaling parameters.

- **Initial Settings**: Define how your Service starts, including the initial number of replicas. This is particularly important for applications expecting immediate traffic upon deployment.

- **Min/Max Replicas (Optional)**: Set boundaries for auto-scaling behavior to ensure that your application scales within expected limits. Knative uses scaling parameters like minScale and maxScale to ensure that the product-listing service can efficiently handle variations in traffic.

```
metadata:
  annotations:
    autoscaling.knative.dev/minScale: 1
    autoscaling.knative.dev/maxScale: 10

```

Listing 4.4: Service definition

4.2.4 Networking: Knative Handles the Details

Knative abstracts the networking layer, simplifying both internal and external communication:

- **Internal Communication**: By default, Knative Services are assigned internal DNS names, facilitating service discovery and communication within the cluster without additional configuration.

- **External Exposure**: Knative automatically configures networking to expose your Services to external traffic, typically through a LoadBalancer or Ingress controller, ensuring your applications are reachable from outside the Kubernetes cluster.

- **Customization**: For advanced networking needs, Knative can be integrated with service meshes like Istio, offering additional capabilities like fine-grained traffic control and enhanced security features.

In our e-commerce platform, the product-listing service needs to be accessible to other services, such as the shopping cart or recommendation engine. Knative simplifies this internal communication by automatically assigning an internal DNS name to the service. This allows other services within the cluster to discover and interact with the product-listing service seamlessly, without any additional configuration

Here's a complete Knative Service definition for a product listing service with additional considerations discussed above:

```
1  apiVersion: serving.knative.dev/v1
2  kind: Service
3  metadata:
4    name: product-listing
5    annotations:
6      # Observability with Prometheus
7      prometheus.io/scrape: "true"
8      prometheus.io/port: "8080"
9  spec:
10   template:
11     spec:
12       containers:
13       - image: my-registry/product-listing:v1.2.0
14         env:
15         - name: DB_HOST
16           valueFrom:
17             secretKeyRef:
18               name: product-db-credentials
19               key: dbhost
20         - name: FEATURE_X_ENABLED
21           value: "true"
22         ports:
23         - containerPort: 8080
```

Listing 4.5: Complete Service definition

This YAML snippet defines a Knative Service that runs the product-listing application. In this detailed example, the Service specifies the container image and the target port for incoming traffic, alongside environment variables. This setup underscores the simplicity in migrating existing containerized applications to Knative, leveraging Kubernetes fundamentals like container specs and environment variables within a serverless framework.

4.2.5 Managing Services with the 'kn' CLI

The Knative `kn` CLI offers a streamlined and user-friendly way to interact with your Knative Services. It provides simplified commands focused on Knative concepts, often reducing the need to directly manage Kubernetes resources. Let's explore how to use the `kn` CLI for essential Service management tasks.

You can create a service using the kn cli as below. Use additional flags like `-env` to set environment variables.

```
$ kn service create <service-name> --image <image-location> -n
    <namespace>
```

Listing 4.6: List pricing Service revisions

The `kn service` cli command can be used to list, describe, update and delete services.

For the team managing our e-commerce platform, the kn CLI becomes an indispensable tool. They can use commands like `kn service create` to initially deploy the product-listing service, `kn service update` to modify its configuration or deploy new versions, and `kn service scale` to adjust the scaling parameters based on observed traffic patterns. The kn CLI streamlines these management tasks, empowering the team to focus on delivering value to customers rather than wrestling with infrastructure complexities.

4.3 Routes: Controlling Traffic

Routes offer sophisticated traffic management capabilities, greatly surpassing the functionality of traditional Kubernetes Ingress or Load-Balancer services. They enable precise control over the distribution of incoming requests across different Revisions. They enable sophisticated deployment strategies, like canary releases and A/B testing, by splitting traffic based on percentages or other criteria. By specifying traffic splitting rules, you can precisely manage the user experience and test new features under real-world conditions with minimal risk. These features are crucial for deploying modern, user-centric applications that require dynamic traffic routing and management strategies

4.3.1 Understanding Routes in Knative

Routes in Knative are designed to intercept requests to your services and route them to the appropriate Revisions based on predefined criteria such as weights or tags. This functionality enables developers to control user experiences finely and roll out new features gradually and safely.

In our e-commerce application the pricing team is working to update the pricing calculation logic, perhaps to incorporate new discount rules or tax calculations. By leveraging Routes, the team can gradually roll out this update, directing a small percentage of requests to the new version of the pricing service. This allows for real-time monitoring and validation of the new logic without affecting the majority of users.

The pricing team creates a routing definition so that 80% of requests for price calculations are directed to the current stable version of the service (pricing-service-v1), while 20% are routed to a new version (pricing-service-v2). This allows for testing the new version with real traffic while minimizing the impact of any potential issues. The route definition can be defined as below.

```
apiVersion: serving.knative.dev/v1
kind: Route
metadata:
  name: pricing-service-route
spec:
  traffic:
  - percent: 80
    revisionName: pricing-service-v1 # Current stable version
  - percent: 20
    revisionName: pricing-service-v2 # New version with updates
```

Listing 4.7: Basic Route Configuration

4.3.2   Advanced Traffic Management

Effective traffic management is crucial for maintaining high availability and ensuring seamless user experiences in dynamic service environments. In this section, we explore advanced strategies for managing traffic within Knative, focusing on canary releases, blue/green deployments, and tag-based routing.

Canary Releases

Canary releases are a methodical approach to rolling out updates by gradually increasing the exposure of a new version of a service to users.

This strategy is especially valuable in minimizing the impact of potential issues that might not have been caught during testing.

In a canary release, a new version of the service (the 'canary') is introduced alongside the stable running version. Initially, only a small percentage of the traffic is directed to the canary version, allowing teams to monitor its performance and stability before incrementally increasing its exposure.

```
apiVersion: serving.knative.dev/v1
kind: Route
metadata:
  name: canary-release
spec:
  traffic:
  - revisionName: service-v1-stable
    percent: 90
  - revisionName: service-v2-canary
    percent: 10
```

Listing 4.8: Canary Release Configuration

This configuration directs 10% of the traffic to the new version (service-v2-canary), allowing for careful monitoring and adjustment based on real-world usage.

Blue/Green Deployments

Blue/green deployments are a robust strategy for updating applications with minimal downtime and risk. This method involves running two identical environments, one hosting the current version (blue) and one hosting the new version (green).

Traffic is initially routed entirely to the blue environment. Once the green environment is tested and ready, traffic is switched in full, which can be reverted quickly if issues arise. This strategy ensures that there is always a live environment available to users.

```
1 apiVersion: serving.knative.dev/v1
2 kind: Route
3 metadata:
4   name: blue-green-deployment
5 spec:
6   traffic:
7   - revisionName: service-v1-blue
8     percent: 100
```

Listing 4.9: Blue/Green Deployment Configuration

Upon confirmation of the green version's stability, traffic can be shifted as follows:

```
1 spec:
2   traffic:
3   - revisionName: service-v2-green
4     percent: 100
```

Tag-based Routing

Tag-based routing enhances the manageability and readability of routing configurations by allowing developers to assign descriptive tags to specific revisions. This method simplifies the process of managing traffic distributions, especially in complex environments with multiple active revisions.

```
1 apiVersion: serving.knative.dev/v1
```

```
2  kind: Route
3  metadata:
4    name: tag-based-routing
5  spec:
6    traffic:
7    - tag: stable-version
8      revisionName: service-v1
9      percent: 80
10   - tag: beta-version
11     revisionName: service-v2
12     percent: 20
```

Listing 4.10: Tag-based Routing Configuration

By using tags like stable-version and beta-version, teams can quickly understand and modify traffic flows without delving into the specifics of revision names and configurations.

Advanced traffic management techniques such as canary releases, blue/green deployments, and tag-based routing provide teams with powerful tools to ensure that service updates are introduced safely and efficiently. By leveraging these strategies, developers can significantly reduce the risk associated with deploying new service versions, ensuring high availability and a positive user experience.

The strategic implementation of these advanced traffic management techniques empowers development teams to navigate the complexities of modern software deployments with confidence. By embracing canary releases, blue/green deployments, and tag-based routing, organizations can ensure the stability, resilience, and seamless evolution of their applications. However, the effective configuration of Routes extends beyond understanding these strategies; it also necessitates adherence to best practices that ensure optimal performance, reliability, and user experience. The following section delves into these best practices, providing actionable insights to maximize the benefits of Knative's traffic management capabilities.

4.3.3 Best Practices for Route Configuration

Configuring Routes in Knative is a critical task that requires strategic planning and attention to detail to ensure that deployments are both robust and flexible. Here are some key best practices to consider when configuring Routes:

Gradual Rollouts   Use weighted traffic splitting to gradually introduce new changes, monitoring metrics and feedback closely.

```
1  apiVersion: serving.knative.dev/v1
2  kind: Route
3  metadata:
4    name: gradual-rollout
5  spec:
6    traffic:
7    - tag: stable
8      revisionName: pricing-service-v1
9      percent: 80
10   - tag: new-feature
11     revisionName: pricing-service-v2
12     percent: 20
```

Listing 4.11: Example of Gradual Rollout

Monitoring and Metrics   Utilize Knative's integrated monitoring tools to continuously track the impact of routing changes on application performance and user experience. Setting up dashboards to visualize traffic behavior and performance metrics can help you make informed decisions about traffic management.

Reversion Strategy Always prepare a reversion strategy to quickly rollback changes if new deployments cause unexpected issues. By defining Routes that can be easily adjusted to redirect traffic back to stable revisions, you can ensure service continuity and minimize downtime.

```
apiVersion: serving.knative.dev/v1
kind: Route
metadata:
  name: quick-rollback
spec:
  traffic:
  - tag: stable
    revisionName: pricing-service-v1
    percent: 100
```

Listing 4.12: Example of Reversion Strategy

The example YAML configuration demonstrates how to redirect all traffic back to a stable revision (pricing-service-v1) in the event that a newer version (pricing-service-v2) causes issues after deployment. By setting the traffic percent to 100 for the stable version, you effectively disable traffic to the problematic new revision. The ability to quickly adjust Route configurations to shift traffic away from a faulty revision minimizes downtime and potential service disruptions. Since Knative handles these changes dynamically, the update takes effect almost immediately, reducing the impact on end-users.

By utilizing Routes in Knative Serving, developers & platform operators gain fine-grained control over how traffic is distributed among different versions of their applications, enabling safer deployments and innovative testing strategies.

4.4   Revisions: Simplify Change Managemen

Knative introduces a robust mechanism for managing application updates through Revisions, which are immutable snapshots of your application's code and configuration at a specific point in time. These Revisions simplify the rollback process, enhance the tracking and auditing of deployments, and provide a reliable method for managing changes in your service environment.

4.4.1   Concept of Revisions in Knative

Revisions in Knative are automatically created whenever there is a change in a Service's configuration or code.   Each Revision is an immutable snapshot, ensuring that any state of the service can be revisited and deployed without conflicts.   This immutability makes Revisions a cornerstone for reliable and consistent deployments and a safety net that allows developers to revert to previous known-good states with ease.

4.4.2   Revision Lifecycle

A Revision goes through several stages from creation to retirement, each serving a specific purpose in the lifecycle of a service:

- **Creation**: Triggered by changes in the Service's code or configuration, creating a new, immutable snapshot. A new Revision is created whenever you modify your Knative Service's code (typically by updating the container image within its associated Configuration.) or its associated Configuration. This immutability ensures consistent deployment and facilitates rollbacks.

- **Build Integration (Optional)**: Integration with CI/CD tools like Tekton automates the process from code changes to container builds, culminating in the creation of new Revisions.

- **Traffic Allocation**: Utilizes the Route resource to manage how traffic is distributed among active Revisions, supporting techniques like canary releases and A/B testing.

- **Scaling**: Dynamically adjusts the number of Pods to match traffic demands, scaling up during peak times and down to zero during idle periods.

- **Retirement (Optional)**: Older Revisions can be phased out to optimize resource usage, with policies in place to retain essential Revisions as needed.

4.4.3 Managing Revisions with kubectl and kn

Interaction with Revisions is facilitated through Knative's CLI tools, offering a range of commands to manage the lifecycle of Revisions effectively.

```
$ kubectl get revisions -n <namespace>
```

Listing 4.13: Using kubectl to list Revisions

This command lists all Revisions in the specified namespace, providing details such as name, creation timestamp, and associated service.

```
$ kn revisions list
```

Listing 4.14: Using kn to list Revisions

Rollback Scenario: Incorrect Discounting Logic

Consider a scenario where an updated version of a pricing calculation service contains a bug. Here's how you can use Revisions to quickly revert to a stable state:

```
$ kn service update pricing-service --traffic
    pricing-service-00001=100
```

Listing 4.15: Initiating a Rollback with kn

This command redirects all traffic back to the previous, stable Revision, ensuring service continuity and minimizing the impact of the buggy update.

Revisions play a critical role in managing the lifecycle of services in Knative, providing the flexibility to test new features and roll back to previous versions effortlessly. By leveraging Revisions, developers can ensure high availability, enhance service reliability, and maintain a high standard of user experience.

4.5 Configurations: Desired State

In Knative Serving, Configurations act as the blueprints that define the desired state of your Services. They serve as the backbone for defining the desired state of applications deployed within the platform. A Configuration encapsulates crucial details about your application's behavior, including scaling parameters, environment variables, and the container image to be deployed. By modifying a Configuration, you instruct Knative Serving to create a new Revision of your Service, reflecting the updated desired state.

4.5.1 Understanding Configurations

Configurations are central to the deployment and updating process in Knative. They maintain a template for creating and updating revisions. Each time you update a Configuration, Knative Serving automatically generates a new Revision, ensuring that changes are rolled out in a controlled and traceable manner.

```
1  apiVersion: serving.knative.dev/v1
2  kind: Configuration
3  metadata:
4    name: product-service
5  spec:
6    template:
7      spec:
8        containers:
9        - image: gcr.io/example/product-service:v1
10         env:
11         - name: ENV_MODE
12           value: production
```

Listing 4.16: Example of Knative Configuration

This YAML snippet defines a basic configuration for a service, specifying the container image and environment variables.

4.5.2 Key Components of Configurations

Configurations encompass a range of parameters that influence your application's behavior. Let's explore some of the key parameters and their significance:

- **Container Image**: The image field within a Configuration specifies the container image that should be deployed for your Service. This allows you to easily update your application by referencing a new image tag or version.

For the product-listing service, we would specify the location of the container image in a registry accessible to our Kubernetes cluster. Each time we update the image tag, Knative Serving would create a new Revision with the updated code.

- **Environment Variables**: As discussed earlier in the chapter, environment variables provide a flexible way to inject configuration into your application at runtime. Configurations allow you to define these environment variables, making it easy to manage and update them without modifying your application code.

In our e-commerce example, we could use environment variables to store the connection details for the product database, ensuring that the product-listing service can access the necessary data.

- **Scaling Parameters**: These parameters govern how your Service scales in response to incoming traffic. You can define the minimum and maximum number of replicas (pods) that should be running, as well as the target concurrency, which influences how Knative decides when to scale up or down.

For our e-commerce product-listing service, we might set the minScale to 1 to ensure at least one instance is always running, minimizing cold start delays. The maxScale could be set to 10 to prevent excessive resource consumption during peak traffic. The target parameter could be adjusted based on the observed performance of the service under different concurrency levels.

4.5.3 Dynamic Update and Rollback

Knative configurations allow for dynamic updates to services without downtime. When a configuration changes, Knative automatically creates a new revision based on this configuration and can gradually route traffic to it.

```
1  spec:
2    template:
3      spec:
4        containers:
5        - image: gcr.io/example/product-service:v2
```

Listing 4.17: Updating a Configuration

Rollback Scenarios: If an update leads to unexpected issues, Knative allows you to quickly revert to a previous configuration by routing traffic back to a prior revision.

4.5.4 Best Practices for Configuration Management

To ensure robust and reliable service deployments, consider the following best practices for configuration management:

- **Immutability**: Treat configurations as immutable once deployed; any changes should trigger a new revision.

- **Version Control**: Keep configurations under version control to track changes and facilitate rollbacks.

- **Environment Separation**: Use different configurations for different environments (e.g., development, staging, production) to prevent configuration drift.

By effectively managing configurations, developers can ensure that their applications consistently behave as expected in the production environment. Knative's model of separating configuration from the actual running code helps maintain a clean and organized deployment process, enabling easy updates and straightforward rollbacks, thus enhancing overall operational efficiency.

4.6 Conclusion

Throughout this chapter, we have delved into the essential components of Knative ServingServices, Routes, Revisions, and Configurationsand demonstrated how they collectively facilitate the efficient deployment and management of serverless applications on Kubernetes. By integrating these components, Knative Serving not only simplifies the operational complexities traditionally associated with managing applications but also enhances scalability and agility.

- **Simplification of Deployment and Management:** We discussed how Knative Serving automates much of the detailed, manual work involved in deploying and managing applications. This automation frees developers to focus on writing code that delivers business value, rather than managing infrastructure.

- **Scalability and Efficiency:** Knative's ability to dynamically manage the scaling of applicationsfrom scaling up during peak demand to scaling down to zero during idle periodsensures that resources are utilized efficiently, which can lead to cost savings and improved application performance.

- **Innovative Traffic Management:** The advanced traffic routing capabilities provided by Knative Routes allow for sophisticated deployment strategies such as canary releases and blue/green deployments. These strategies enable safer updates and feature rollouts, minimizing the risk of negatively impacting the user experience.

- **Reliable Change Management:** By leveraging Revisions and Configurations, Knative provides a robust framework for managing changes and ensuring that any version of the application can be deployed and rolled back with confidence.

As we progress further into the world of cloud-native computing, the tools and practices provided by Knative will become increasingly essential. The modular and interoperable nature of Knative components allows them to be seamlessly integrated into a variety of development workflows and cloud environments, offering organizations the flexibility to adapt to new challenges and opportunities in the technology landscape.

Looking Ahead: In subsequent chapters, we will explore more advanced topics, including deeper integrations with cloud-native ecosystems, building and deploying multi-component applications, and leveraging the full power of the Kubernetes platform in conjunction with Knative.

With these foundations in place, we are now ready to explore advanced Knative Serving features, including traffic management, security, and progressive deployments. In the next chapter, we will dive deeper into Knative Serving's advanced capabilities, equipping you with the tools needed to manage production-ready serverless applications.

5

Advanced Knative Serving

... The Web does not just connect machines, it connects people.

(Tim Berners-Lee)

How do you manage high-traffic workloads without downtime? What if you could gradually roll out new updates to only a fraction of users, testing features in real-time before a full deployment? How do you secure serverless applications while maintaining performance and observability? In this chapter, we go beyond the basics and explore advanced Knative Serving capabilitiesfrom complex traffic management strategies to service mesh integrations and performance optimization. Building on the fundamentals from Chapter 4, we will now tackle real-world challenges, ensuring that your serverless applications are resilient, scalable, and production-ready.

In the previous chapters, particularly in Chapter 4, we laid a solid foundation by introducing you to the essentials of Knative Serving. We explored its core components Services, Routes, Revisions, and Configurations and how they work together to deploy and manage serverless applications efficiently on Kubernetes. As we transition from the foundational concepts, it is now time to challenge these concepts under more demanding scenarios and explore their advanced capabilities. This chapter not only extends the operational skills but also deepens the strategic understanding necessary for deploying and managing sophisticated serverless architectures on Kubernetes.

By the end of this chapter, you will:

- ► Implement advanced traffic management strategies to improve application responsiveness and control.
- ► Integrate Knative with service meshes for enhanced security, observability, and networking capabilities.
- ► Optimize configuration and revision management for continuous deployment in dynamic environments.
- ► Monitor and enhance the performance of serverless applications to maximize efficiency and scalability.

Through detailed explanations and practical examples, this chapter will guide you through configuring complex deployment patterns, integrating cutting-edge security practices, and leveraging powerful monitoring tools. You'll learn how to harness the full potential of Knative to manage modern serverless applications effectively. Let's embark on this advanced journey to unlock the next level of serverless computing with Knative Serving.

5.1 Advanced Traffic Management

In Chapter 4, *Knative Serving Essentials*, we explored the fundamentals of traffic management in Knative, focusing on basic routing and traffic splitting between different revisions of a service. Building upon this foundation, we will now explore how Knative implements a pluggable architecture to incorporate advanced networking and ingress components enabling the implementation of sophisticated traffic management strategies.

In serverless architectures, the role of networking extends beyond simple connectivity; it becomes a pivotal component in routing, scaling, and securing applications dynamically. Knative Serving embraces this complexity through a pluggable networking architecture that allows users to seamlessly integrate a variety of networking solutions, tailoring the environment to meet their operational needs.

Knative's pluggable architecture provides the framework's capability to seamlessly accommodate a spectrum of networking layers and ingress controllers, underpinned by a uniform set of APIs and configuration structures. This architectural design facilitates effortless component swapping without necessitating extensive modifications to the deployment or application codebase. It enables organizations to choose between components such as Istio, Kourier, Ambassador, Gloo and others. Organizations can tailor solutions based on performance, security features, and other requirements allowing them to adapt to diverse cloud environments and infrastructure requirements. This pluggable design is not just about flexibility today; it's about future-proofing your serverless investments by preventing vendor lock-in. You are free to choose the networking solution that best fits your needs, and you can evolve your infrastructure over time without being tied to a single, proprietary stack. Knative's commitment to open standards and pluggability ensures long-term adaptability and control over your serverless environment.

Knative's pluggable architecture is implemented through its Custom Resource Definitions (CRDs). These CRDs encapsulate the vital information required to manage serverless applications while serving as the backbone of Knative's flexible networking and ingress capabilities. This design allows Knative to seamlessly integrate with a multitude of networking layers, showcasing its adaptability to various operational environments and requirements.

5.1.1 Core CRDs and Their Roles

- *Service* : The Service CRD in Knative is the high-level entry point for managing a serverless workload. It abstracts away the complexity of lower-level components such as configurations, routes, and revisions. It automatically manages the entire lifecycle of an application, including networking aspects like creating and updating routes and managing traffic policies. When a Service is updated, Knative automatically updates other related CRDs like Route and Configuration, which in turn may update networking rules in the chosen ingress solution (e.g., creating or modifying Istio's VirtualServices).

- *Route*: The Route CRD manages how traffic is routed to different Revisions of a service within Knative. It is central to the traffic management capabilities of Knative. It defines rules for splitting traffic between different revisions based on percentages or user-defined conditions. Route works by interfacing with the ingress controller's routing capabilities, such as Istio's VirtualService or Kourier's direct Envoy configuration. Changes in Route translate into updates in these ingress resources, which handle the actual traffic splitting.

- *Configuration* : This CRD holds the desired state of the deployment and is responsible for creating and maintaining immutable Revision resources whenever the configuration changes. It ensures that every change to the application's code or configuration triggers a new Revision, allowing rollbacks and version control. The Configuration CRD impacts how traffic is managed by triggering updates in Revisions, which are then referenced by Routes.

- *Revision*: The Revision CRD represents an immutable snapshot of application code and configuration at a specific point in time. Each Revision is a deployable entity that can be independently scaled and managed. It maintains the history of changes and can be specifically targeted by Routes. Revisions are the endpoints that ingress controllers direct traffic to, based on the rules defined in Routes. They are crucial for ensuring that the right version of the application responds to specific requests.

These four Core CRDs — Service, Route, Configuration, and Revision — work in concert to provide a declarative and powerful foundation for managing every aspect of your serverless application lifecycle within Knative, with traffic management as a central, dynamically configurable element. They encapsulate the necessary information for managing serverless applications and form the backbone of Knative's pluggable architecture for networking and ingress.

5.1.2 How CRDs Support Pluggable Architecture

The above Knative CRDs not only encapsulate the necessary information for managing serverless applications but also form the backbone of its pluggable architecture for networking and ingress. This detailed design enables Knative to seamlessly integrate with a variety of networking layers, demonstrating the platform's flexibility and adaptability to different operational environments and requirements. They enable its pluggable architecture through

- *Decoupling of Concerns*: By separating traffic management (Route), application configuration (Configuration), and deployment snapshots (Revision) into different CRDs, Knative allows each aspect of the serverless application to be managed independently. This separation is crucial for integrating different networking solutions that can handle specific parts of the traffic and configuration lifecycle.

- *Interchangeability of Networking Solutions*: Each networking layer that integrates with Knative interacts with these CRDs through a defined set of APIs. For instance, changing from Istio to Kourier primarily involves how these CRDs are interpreted and acted upon by the ingress controller, without altering the CRDs themselves. This design allows users to plug in different networking solutions according to their performance, complexity, and feature requirements.

- *Uniform API Surface*: Regardless of the underlying networking solution, the API exposed by Knative CRDs remains consistent. This consistency ensures that the user experience does not change when swapping out one ingress controller for another, facilitating ease of use and reducing learning curves.

By strategically decoupling concerns and providing a uniform API through its CRDs, Knative's pluggable architecture not only simplifies integration with diverse networking solutions but also ensures future adaptability and avoids vendor lock-in, making it a robust foundation for evolving serverless environments. By understanding the roles and interactions of these CRDs, you gain a deeper appreciation for how Knative's pluggable architecture allows you to tailor your networking and ingress to perfectly suit your needs. This intricate orchestration of the Service, Route, Configuration, and Revision CRDs creates a powerful synergy, providing a unified and highly adaptable system for managing serverless applications.

5.1.3 Networking and Ingress options

Some of the popular ingress and networking options for Knative are

- *Istio*: Initially, Istio was the default for Knative, offering advanced traffic management, security, and observability. It is still widely used due to its robust feature set.

- *Kourier*: Designed specifically for Knative as a lightweight alternative to Istio, focusing solely on serving as an ingress for Knative to improve performance and simplicity. Kourier is laser-focused on efficiently serving as the ingress layer for Knative, offering a significantly less resource-intensive footprint compared to Istio. It can be an excellent choice when advanced service mesh features are not immediately required and a streamlined, fast ingress solution is paramount for your Knative deployments. Kourier is built using Envoy Proxy as its core, leveraging Envoy's performance but with a configuration and operational model simplified for Knative's specific needs.

- *Contour*: Utilizes Envoy as the ingress controller, known for its performance and ease of configuration. It provides a simpler yet powerful alternative for handling ingress.

- *Gloo*: An API gateway built on Envoy that supports Knative by providing advanced routing, security, and integration capabilities.

- *Ambassador*: Another Envoy-based solution that acts as both an API gateway and an ingress controller, tailored for microservices architectures and integrated with Knative.

It's important to note that while Knative's pluggable architecture supports a variety of ingress controllers, the level of "advanced traffic management" features available can vary significantly between them. Choosing the right ingress controller depends on the specific requirements of your application and the level of advanced networking features you need to leverage. For instance, Istio, as highlighted in this chapter, generally offers the most comprehensive suite of advanced capabilities, including contextual routing, mutual TLS policy enforcement, and detailed observability. Other ingress options may prioritize different aspects, such as simplicity or performance, and might offer a more streamlined set of features focused primarily on basic ingress functionality. Based on this, lets explore a concrete example, showcasing how Knative Custom Resource Definitions (CRDs) align with Istio resources to enable advanced traffic management, enhanced security, and comprehensive observability.

5.1.4 Istio for Ingress and Networking

Istio is a comprehensive service mesh that offers advanced traffic management, robust security features, and detailed observability. When integrated with Knative, Istio provides these capabilities at the ingress level and internally within the cluster. However, service meshes like Istio are known for their complexity. Knative expertly simplifies the adoption and management of Istio in a serverless context. It abstracts away much of the intricate Istio configuration, allowing you to leverage its powerful features for advanced traffic management, security, and observability without the steep learning curve typically associated with service meshes. Knative makes Istio's advanced capabilities accessible and manageable for serverless workloads.

CRD Mapping and Implementation

Integrating Istio with Knative not only enhances the ingress capabilities but also significantly boosts internal service management and security. As shown in Figure 5.1, the seamless mapping of CRDs between Knative and Istio showcases the strength of Knative's pluggable architecture, enabling comprehensive traffic management, enhanced security, and detailed observability across serverless applications. This practical integration allows developers and operators to leverage the best of both platforms, optimizing their Kubernetes environments for performance and scalability.

The architectural relationship depicted in Figure 5.1 emphasizes the dynamic interaction between Knative components, such as Services and Routes, and their corresponding Istio configurations, such as VirtualServices. This relationship ensures that changes made at the Knative layer automatically propagate to Istio, enabling advanced traffic management strategies and seamless updates.

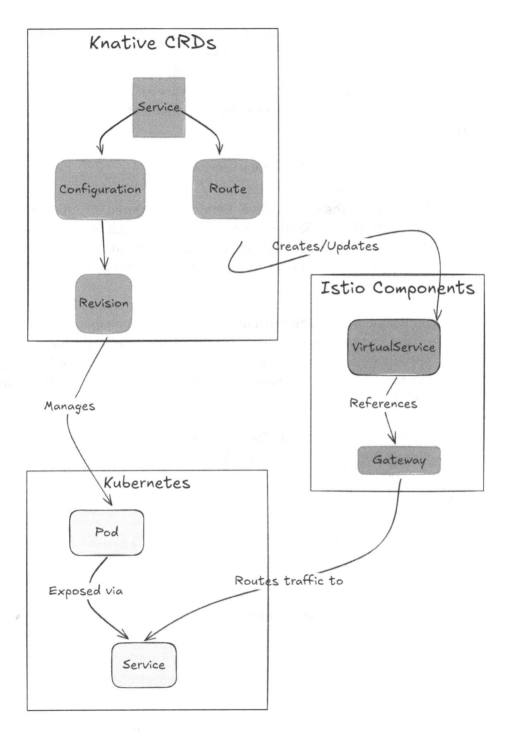

Figure 5.1: Knative CRDs and Istio components

To understand this relationship in greater detail, let us consider the mapping and implementation of the key components. We will also look at a basic sample implementation. This will provide the foundational knowledge needed to delve into even more specialized capabilities, such as contextual routing, which uses request metadata to make dynamic routing decisions.

1. Knative Service and Istio VirtualService

- *Mapping*: When a Knative Service is created or updated, it automatically configures a Knative Route, which in turn triggers the creation of an Istio VirtualService. This illustrates the dynamic interaction between Knative and Istio, highlighting the responsiveness of the system to changes.

- *Implementation*: The VirtualService directly manages the routing of traffic to the appropriate Knative Revisions, according to the specifications in the Route. This setup facilitates advanced routing strategies such as header-based routing, traffic splitting, and URL path-based decisions.

- *Example Configuration*: The following YAML snippet demonstrates how a VirtualService is defined to route traffic between two versions of a service based on a URL prefix

```
1   apiVersion: networking.istio.io/v1alpha3
2   kind: VirtualService
3   metadata:
4     name: myservice-virtualservice
5   spec:
6     hosts:
7       - myservice.example.com
8     http:
9       - match:
10          - uri:
11              prefix: /v1
```

```
12      route:
13        - destination:
14            host:
        myservice-v1.knative-serving.svc.cluster.local
15            weight: 90
16        - destination:
17            host:
        myservice-v2.knative-serving.svc.cluster.local
18            weight: 10
19
```

Listing 5.1: Service definition

2. Knative Route and Istio Gateway

- *Mapping*: The Route specifies which revisions should receive traffic, translating this specification into Istio's Gateway and VirtualService resources to manage ingress traffic.

- *Implementation*: The Gateway resource defines the entry points for traffic entering the cluster, while the VirtualService specifies how this traffic is routed to the correct destinations within the cluster.

- *Example Configuration*: The following YAML snippet demonstrates how a Gateway is defined to route traffic to a Knative Service based on a specific host

```
1   apiVersion: networking.istio.io/v1alpha3
2   kind: Gateway
3   metadata:
4     name: myservice-gateway
5   spec:
6     selector:
7       istio: ingressgateway
8     servers:
9     - port:
10        number: 80
```

```
11      name: http
12      protocol: HTTP
13    hosts:
14    - myservice.example.com
15
```

Listing 5.2: Service definition

3. Security with Istio's PeerAuthentication

- *Mapping*: Security configurations in Istio, such as PeerAuthentication, enforce mutual TLS between services, aligning with security policies specified at the Knative Service level.

- *Implementation*: Ensures that all traffic between services is encrypted and authenticated at the service mesh level.

- *Example Configuration*: The following YAML snippet demonstrates how PeerAuthentication is defined to enforce mutual TLS between services

```
1  apiVersion: security.istio.io/v1
2  kind: PeerAuthentication
3  metadata:
4    name: default
5    namespace: knative-serving
6  spec:
7    mtls:
8      mode: STRICT
9
```

Listing 5.3: Service definition

4. Observability with Istio

Effective observability is essential for maintaining the performance, reliability, and health of serverless applications. Istio's built-in telemetry tools provide a comprehensive suite of metrics, logs, and traces that allow you to monitor services integrated with Knative. By leveraging these tools, developers and operators can gain deep insights into application behavior and quickly identify and resolve potential bottle-necks or issues. The seamless integration of Istio's comprehensive traffic management, robust security, and detailed observability features with Knative's serverless platform creates a remarkable synergy. This powerful combination empowers developers to build highly scalable, secure, and deeply observable serverless applications on Kubernetes, leveraging the best of both ecosystems.

- *Mapping*: Istio automatically collects detailed telemetry data for all traffic within the service mesh, including metrics, logs, and distributed traces. These data points provide a clear picture of how services interact, the performance of requests, and any anomalous behavior in the application flow.

- *Visualization*: Tools like Kiali, Grafana, and Jaeger are seamlessly integrated with Istio to offer actionable visualizations:

  - **Kiali**: Provides a service graph for understanding traffic flow and dependencies between microservices.

  - **Grafana**: Enables the creation of customized dashboards to track performance metrics such as latency, request through-put, and error rates.

  - **Jaeger**: Delivers distributed tracing capabilities, helping pinpoint the root cause of latency issues or failures across service interactions.

- *Example Configuration*: The following YAML snippet demonstrates how to enable Istio's telemetry features for monitoring service interactions

```
1   apiVersion: install.istio.io/v1alpha1
2   kind: IstioOperator
3   spec:
4     components:
5       prometheus:
6         enabled: true
7       grafana:
8         enabled: true
9       tracing:
10        enabled: true
11
```

Listing 5.4: Service definition

In summary, integrating Istio with Knative is a strategic enhancement that leverages the strengths of both platforms. Istio provides the advanced networking, security, and observability infrastructure, while Knative orchestrates and simplifies the deployment and management of serverless applications on top of it. This powerful combination provides a robust and feature-rich environment for running production-ready, scalable, and secure serverless workloads.

Now that we have understood these relationships and implementations, we can delve into more specialized use cases, such as contextual routing, which leverages request metadata to enable dynamic and highly personalized routing decisions.

5.1.5 Contextual Routing

Contextual routing refers to the ability to route requests based on the context provided by request headers, cookies, or other environmental variables. This allows for a highly personalized user experience and can be critical for applications requiring dynamic content delivery or user-specific responses. Our e-commerce platform wants to present a personalized product catalog based on the user's browsing history or location. With Istio's contextual routing capabilities, you can direct requests to different versions of your product catalog service, each tailored to specific user segments.

How It Works

Integrated with Knative, Istio provides dynamic routing capabilities by defining virtual services and destination rules that route traffic based on specific conditions.

Practical Implementation

- **Setup:** Ensure Istio is properly integrated with Knative.

- **Configuration:** Apply the following YAML to define a VirtualService for contextual routing:

```
 1  apiVersion: networking.istio.io/v1alpha3
 2  kind: VirtualService
 3  metadata:
 4    name: contextual-routing
 5  spec:
 6    hosts:
 7    - your-service.your-domain.com
 8    http:
 9    - match:
10      - headers:
11          user-type:
12            exact: premium
13      route:
14      - destination:
15          host: premium-service
16    - route:
```

```
17      - destination:
18          host: standard-service
19
```

Listing 5.5: Istio VirtualService Configuration for Contextual Routing

This configuration implements a header-based routing strategy and directs traffic based on the user-type header.

Use Cases

Examples include A/B testing and delivering personalized content based on user data.

5.2 Integration with Service Meshes

In today's complex cloud-native landscapes, service meshes, and notably Istio, have evolved from optional enhancements to essential infrastructure for managing and securing microservices communication. As your serverless applications scale and become more intricate, managing their internal network becomes paramount for both reliability and security. For Knative, which excels at simplifying serverless deployments on Kubernetes, integration with a service mesh like Istio is not just an option — it's a strategic upgrade. This section will demonstrate how this powerful convergence not only significantly enhances Knative's traffic management and security features but also unlocks a new level of robustness and operational control for your serverless architectures.

5.2.1 Unlocking the Benefits

Service mesh integration enriches Knative with several pivotal advantages:

- **Advanced Traffic Management**: Istio extends Knative's routing capabilities with sophisticated load balancing algorithms (like least request or ring hash) and precise traffic splitting for implementing detailed canary releases and A/B testing strategies. These features facilitate dynamic traffic management based on a variety of criteria, including HTTP headers, cookies, and user identities.

- **Robust Security Measures**: By implementing mutual TLS (mTLS), Istio secures all in-cluster communications between services, ensuring data integrity and confidentiality. Furthermore, Istio's comprehensive policy enforcement allows for defining detailed access controls, enhancing the security posture beyond Knative's default capabilities.

- **Enhanced Observability**: Istio provides extensive monitoring tools that offer deep visibility into the metrics and logs of service interactions. This observability is crucial for proactive performance tuning and quick troubleshooting, enabling developers to maintain high service standards in production.

- **Operational Flexibility**: With Istio, developers can utilize an array of traffic management and security features without modifying their application code. This separation of concerns ensures that developers can focus on business logic, while operational aspects like routing and security are managed externally.

- **Scalability and Resilience**: Features such as circuit breakers and rate limiting in Istio help manage service reliability and resource utilization efficiently, preventing service degradation during high traffic events or attacks, thus supporting Knative's scalability promises.

Knative and Istio together provide a robust framework for deploying and managing serverless and microservices architectures efficiently. Understanding how these technologies interact helps in leveraging their strengths for traffic management, service scalability, and security. Through these pivotal benefits, service mesh integration fundamentally transforms Knative, elevating it from a serverless deployment platform to a comprehensive environment for building, securing, and operating sophisticated, enterprise-grade serverless applications.

5.2.2 Internal Traffic Distribution and Auto-Scaling

Knative excels in managing internal traffic distribution and auto-scaling of services:

- **Knative Serving**: Automatically scales the number of pods up or down based on traffic patterns. It uses a built-in autoscaler which reacts to incoming request rates and adjusts the number of active pods accordingly.

- **Traffic Splitting**: Allows developers to route traffic between different revisions of an application based on predefined rules, enabling canary releases and A/B testing without external tools.

Knative's automatic internal traffic distribution and intelligent auto-scaling features demonstrate a powerful synergy. Traffic Splitting allows for controlled rollouts and testing of new versions, while auto-scaling ensures that resources are dynamically adjusted to meet the actual traffic demands directed by these sophisticated routing strategies. This combined capability allows for both agility in deployments and efficiency in resource utilization.

Example: Knative Service Configuration for Traffic Management

```
1  apiVersion: serving.knative.dev/v1
2  kind: Service
3  metadata:
4    name: product-service
5  spec:
6    template:
7      spec:
8        containers:
9        - image: product-service:v2
10   traffic:
11   - tag: current
12     revisionName: product-service-v1
13     percent: 50
14   - tag: candidate
15     revisionName: product-service-v2
16     percent: 50
```

Listing 5.6: Knative Service Configuration for Traffic Splitting

This configuration demonstrates how Knative manages traffic between two versions of a service, enabling gradual rollouts of new features.

5.2.3 External Traffic - Kubernetes LoadBalancer

For external traffic management, Kubernetes provides the LoadBalancer service type, which exposes services outside the cluster. This is particularly useful for production environments where where high availability and external accessibility are critical. The LoadBalancer service type provisions a cloud provider's load balancer to route external traffic to the service, ensuring high availability and scalability. However, it's important to distinguish between Kubernetes LoadBalancer Services and Ingress Controllers. The LoadBalancer service operates at Layer 4 (Transport Layer) of the OSI model, primarily handling TCP/UDP traffic and providing basic load balancing. Ingress Controllers, like Istio's Gateway or Kourier, operate at Layer 7 (Application Layer), and are designed for HTTP/HTTPS traffic, enabling much more sophisticated application-level routing, such as path-based routing, header-based routing, TLS termination, and other advanced traffic management features discussed in this chapter. While a LoadBalancer makes your service externally accessible, Ingress Controllers offer the advanced, application-aware traffic management capabilities often needed for modern web applications and microservices.

Example: Kubernetes Service with LoadBalancer

```
apiVersion: v1
kind: Service
metadata:
  name: external-loadbalancer
spec:
  type: LoadBalancer
  selector:
    app: product-service
  ports:
    - protocol: TCP
      port: 80
      targetPort: 8080
```

Listing 5.7: Kubernetes LoadBalancer Configuration

This configuration sets up a LoadBalancer to handle incoming external traffic, directing it to the appropriate pods based on the selector criteria.

5.2.4 Advanced Traffic Management with Istio

Istio complements Knative by providing advanced traffic management capabilities and enhanced security features , as illustrated in Figure 5.2

- **Fine-Grained Traffic Control**: Istio offers sophisticated routing rules, retries, failovers, and fault injection for robust traffic management.

- **Security with Mutual TLS**: Enhances security by encrypting and authenticating traffic between services, which is vital in a multi-tenant environment.

Example: Istio VirtualService for Advanced Routing

The sequence shown in Figure 5.2 is enabled by Istio's VirtualService configuration. Below is a concrete example implementing URI-based routing:

```
apiVersion: networking.istio.io/v1
kind: VirtualService
metadata:
  name: product-vservice
spec:
  hosts:
    - product-service.example.com
  http:
    - match:
        - uri:
            prefix: /v2
      route:
        - destination:
            host: product-service-v2.default.svc.cluster.local
            port:
```

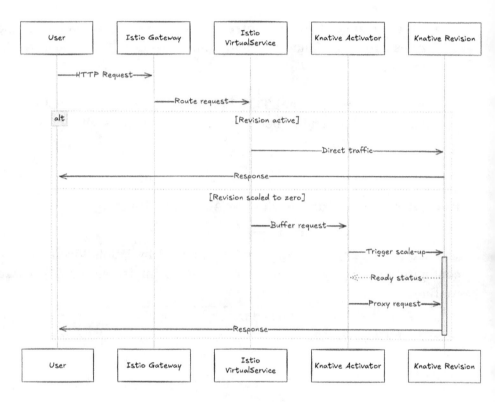

Figure 5.2: Integrated traffic flow - Istio and Knative

```
16              number: 8080
```

Listing 5.8: Istio VirtualService Configuration for Advanced Routing

This configuration directly correlates with the routing decision point in Figure 5.2, where the VirtualService inspects the request URI before directing traffic. The `prefix:    /v2` match condition determines whether requests follow the active revision path or require activator intervention during scale-up events.

- **Active Revision Path: Traffic to Existing Pods**: Matches requests to pre-scaled instances of `product-service-v2`. When traffic arrives for the `/v2` prefix, and instances of `product-service-v2` are already running (scaled up), the VirtualService directly routes these requests to those existing pods. This represents the "active revision path" for normal, scaled-up operation. The VirtualService ensures efficient routing to available instances.

- **Scale-Up Path: Handling Cold Starts via Knative Activator**: Handles scenarios where `product-service-v2` is initially scaled to zero (cold start). If no pods of `product-service-v2` are running when a request for `/v2` arrives, the VirtualService, in conjunction with Knative, will initially route the request to the Knative Activator component. The Activator acts as a proxy and holds the incoming request while Knative auto-scaling spins up new pods for `product-service-v2`. Once pods are ready, the Activator forwards the held request to the newly scaled-up revision. This process, though involving the Activator, is transparent to the user and ensures seamless scale-up from zero.

- **Port Mapping**: Aligns with the service endpoints shown in the diagram. The `port.number:    8080` in the VirtualService configuration specifies the port on which the `product-service-v2` pods are listening for traffic, ensuring correct communication between the ingress and the backend service.

Istio's VirtualService, as demonstrated, provides a declarative and powerful way to implement fine-grained traffic control within your Knative environment, going far beyond basic routing and enabling sophisticated deployment strategies and request handling.

5.3 Monitoring & Performance Optimization

In the realm of serverless computing, where resources are dynamically allocated and scaled, keeping a watchful eye on your Knative applications is crucial. Effective monitoring empowers you to detect performance bottlenecks, ensure optimal resource utilization, and troubleshoot issues promptly. In this section, we'll explore the tools and techniques that enable you to achieve these goals, turning raw metrics into actionable insights.

5.3.1 Essential Knative Monitoring Tools

Knative, along with its integration with the Kubernetes ecosystem, offers a powerful toolkit for monitoring your serverless applications. Setting up comprehensive monitoring for microservices can often be a complex and time-consuming task. Knative, in conjunction with standard Kubernetes monitoring tools, offers comprehensive observability practically out-of-the-box for your serverless applications, significantly reducing operational burden. You gain immediate visibility into your services with pre-integrated metrics, logs, and tracing capabilities, allowing you to focus on application development and innovation rather than spending cycles on building complex monitoring infrastructure from scratch. Let's dive into some of the key components:

1. **Prometheus and Grafana:**

   - **Prometheus**, the de facto monitoring solution for Kubernetes, collects metrics from various sources, including Knative components and your application itself.

   - **Grafana**, a versatile visualization platform, allows you to create insightful dashboards and graphs to visualize Prometheus metrics. This combination provides a comprehensive overview of your Knative application's health and performance.

2. **Knative's Built-in Metrics:**

   - Knative itself exposes a rich set of metrics that offer valuable insights into the behavior of your serverless workloads.

   - These metrics include:

       - **Request count and latency:** Track the number of requests handled by your services and the time taken to process them.

       - **Scaling events:** Monitor how Knative scales your services up or down in response to traffic patterns.

       - **Resource utilization:** Understand how your services are consuming CPU, memory, and other resources.

3. **Logging and Tracing:**

   - Centralized logging solutions like **Elasticsearch, Fluentd, and Kibana (EFK)** or cloud-native logging platforms can capture and analyze logs from your Knative applications. To enable logging aggregation, you typically need to deploy a logging agent (like Fluentd or Fluent Bit) to collect logs from your Knative pods and forward them to a backend like Elasticsearch or Grafana Loki. Cloud-managed Kubernetes services often provide integrated logging solutions that can be easily configured.

- Distributed tracing tools like **Jaeger** or **OpenTelemetry** can help you trace requests as they flow through your Knative services, providing end-to-end visibility into your application's behavior. To get started with tracing, you would typically deploy a tracing backend like Jaeger or Zipkin in your cluster and configure your Knative services to propagate trace context. Knative, especially when integrated with a service mesh like Istio, simplifies trace context propagation by automatically injecting necessary headers into requests.

5.3.2 Interpreting Metrics for Optimal Performance

Once you have the right monitoring tools in place, it's essential to understand the key metrics and how to interpret them to identify potential performance issues.

- **High Request Latency:** If your services are experiencing consistently high request latency, it could indicate bottlenecks in your application code, network congestion, or resource constraints.

- **Frequent Scaling Events:** While Knative's auto-scaling is a powerful feature, frequent scaling events could suggest that your application is not scaling efficiently or that there are sudden spikes in traffic that need to be addressed.

- **High Resource Utilization:** If your services are consistently consuming a high percentage of available CPU or memory, it might be time to consider scaling up your deployments or optimizing your application code.

5.3.3 Performance & Cost Optimization

Monitoring provides the insights you need to take proactive steps to optimize your Knative applications for both performance and cost-efficiency.

- **Code Optimization:** Profiling your code and identifying performance hotspots can lead to significant improvements in response times and resource utilization.

- **Concurrency Control:** Carefully managing concurrency in your Go services can prevent them from becoming overwhelmed under heavy load, leading to improved performance and stability. In Knative Serving, you can control concurrency at the Revision level using the `containerConcurrency` setting. Setting an appropriate value for `containerConcurrency` ensures that each pod instance can handle a reasonable number of concurrent requests without becoming overloaded. This prevents request queuing and reduces latency, especially under high traffic. Refer to Chapter 6 for a detailed discussion on Revision management and concurrency settings.

- **Efficient Auto-scaling:** Fine-tune Knative's auto-scaling configuration to ensure your services scale up and down quickly and efficiently in response to traffic patterns, balancing performance and cost.

- **Resource Allocation:** Analyze your resource utilization metrics to identify opportunities for right-sizing your Knative deployments, avoiding over-provisioning while ensuring adequate resources are available to handle peak loads. When defining your Knative Services, you can specify resource `requests` and `limits` in the pod spec (within the Service YAML). `requests` guarantee a minimum amount of resources (CPU, memory) for each pod, while `limits` set the maximum resources a pod can consume. By analyzing metrics, you can adjust these `requests` and `limits` to match your service's actual needs, optimizing resource usage and cost. For example, if your service consistently uses only 50% of its requested CPU, you can safely reduce the `requests.cpu` value.

Monitoring and performance optimization are not independent activities; they are deeply interconnected. Effective monitoring provides the crucial data and actionable insights that fuel targeted performance optimization strategies. This complementary relationship allows for a continuous cycle of improvement, leading to serverless applications that are not only performant but also cost-efficient and resilient in the face of varying demands.

5.3.4 Troubleshooting Performance Issues

Let's consider a hypothetical scenario where you're experiencing high request latency in your `order-service`. You begin your investigation by observing your Grafana dashboards, specifically looking at metrics for the `order-service`. In your Grafana dashboard, you observe the following:

- **High CPU Utilization:** The `order-service` is consistently consuming a high percentage of available CPU resources, as shown in your Grafana CPU utilization dashboard for this service.

- **Slow Database Queries (Identified via Tracing):** To investigate the high CPU, you utilize distributed tracing. Examining traces for slow requests to the `order-service` using Jaeger reveals that database queries within the `order-service` spans are taking a significant amount of time.

To further understand the slow database queries, you delve into your application logs using a logging system like EFK. Analyzing the logs (correlated by trace ID if possible, or by timestamp around the time of slow requests) reveals detailed logs from the `order-service` indicating specific slow-running SQL queries and potential database connection issues.

Based on these observations, gathered from your monitoring and observability tools, you could take the following steps to troubleshoot and address the performance issue:

1. **Optimize Database Queries:** Review and optimize the database queries within your `order-service` code to improve their efficiency.

2. **Database Indexing:** Ensure appropriate indexes are in place on the database tables used by the `order-service`, as potential missing indexes might be contributing to the slow query performance observed in traces and logs.

3. **Scale Up:** If query optimization and indexing don't fully resolve the issue, and Grafana continues to show high CPU utilization even after query improvements, consider scaling up the `order-service` deployment to provide additional CPU resources.

5.3.5 Enabling Prometheus and Knative Integration

Knative Serving has built-in support for Prometheus as a metrics backend, making it simple to integrate and gain immediate insights into your services. This integration is primarily configured through the `config-observability` ConfigMap, which serves as the central configuration point for observability settings in Knative. While this section focuses on Prometheus integration for metrics, the `config-observability` ConfigMap also plays a crucial role in configuring logging and tracing destinations for Knative components, as we will discuss further in Chapter 9.4.

Follow these steps to enable Prometheus metrics collection for Knative Serving:

1. **Ensure Prometheus is Deployed:**

   - If you haven't already, deploy Prometheus in your Kubernetes cluster. The Prometheus Operator simplifies this process by providing custom resource definitions and controllers for managing Prometheus deployments.For basic monitoring, a simple Prometheus deployment is sufficient. For production environments, consider a more robust and scalable Prometheus setup, potentially using the Prometheus Operator for lifecycle management and high availability.

2. **Configure Knative to Use Prometheus via `config-observability` ConfigMap:**

   - Edit the `config-observability` ConfigMap in the knative-serving namespace. This ConfigMap controls how Knative components export metrics, logs, and traces.

```
kubectl edit configmap config-observability -n
knative-serving
```

- Within the `config-observability` ConfigMap's data section, set the `metrics.request-metrics-backend-destination` property to `prometheus`:

```
1    data:
2
     metrics.request-metrics-backend-destination:
     prometheus
3
```

This setting instructs Knative Serving components to export request metrics in a format that Prometheus can scrape.

- **Save the changes.** Kubernetes will automatically update the Knative Serving components to apply the new configuration in the `config-observability` ConfigMap.

3. **(Optional) Deploy the Knative Monitoring Resources:**

- If you're using the Knative Operator, it usually deploys the necessary monitoring resources, including ServiceMonitors, automatically. ServiceMonitors are Kubernetes resources that tell Prometheus how to discover and scrape metrics endpoints from services within the cluster.

- If not using the Operator, or for more customized metric collection, you might need to manually deploy the `knative-monitoring` resources. These resources typically include ServiceMonitors pre-configured to discover and scrape metrics from Knative components. Deploying these resources ensures that Prometheus can effectively discover and collect all the built-in Knative metrics, providing a richer observability experience. You can often find these knative-monitoring resources in the Knative release manifests or example repositories.

After completing these steps, Prometheus will be configured to scrape metrics from your Knative Serving deployments. You can then use Grafana, as discussed in Section 5.3.5, to visualize these metrics and gain insights into your serverless application's performance and health.

5.3.6 Performing Queries to Get the Right Informatio

Once the integration is set up, you can harness the power of Prometheus's query language (PromQL) to extract valuable insights into your Knative applications. To effectively visualize these insights, you can use Grafana to create dashboards that display the metrics collected by Prometheus. The example Grafana dashboard below illustrates how metrics obtained from PromQL queries can be visualized to gain an at-a-glance understanding of your Knative services' performance and health.

Let's explore some illustrative queries:

1. **Request Count and Latency:**

   - **Total requests handled by a specific Knative service:**

   ```
   sum(knative_request_count{destination_service =
       "your-service-name"})
   ```

- **Average request latency for a service:**

```
sum(knative_request_latencies_sum{destination_service
    = "your-service-name"})
/
sum(knative_request_count{destination_service =
    "your-service-name"})
```

2. **Scaling Events:**

- **Number of times a service scaled up in the last hour:**

```
count_over_time(knative_revision_autoscaling_events
{reason="scale_up", destination_service =
    "your-service-name"}[1h])
```

3. **Resource Utilization:**

- **Average CPU usage of a service's pods:**

```
avg(rate(container_cpu_usage_seconds_total
{container != "POD", pod = ~"your-service-name-.*"
    }[1m]))
```

- **Memory usage of a service's pods:**

```
sum(container_memory_usage_bytes
{container != "POD", pod=~ "your-service-name-.*" })
```

These queries provide a glimpse into the rich insights you can derive from Prometheus metrics. By visualizing these metrics in Grafana dashboards, you can gain a comprehensive understanding of your Knative services' performance, scalability, and resource utilization, enabling you to make informed decisions to optimize your serverless applications.

5.4 Conclusion

In this chapter, we ventured into the advanced aspects of Knative Serving, showcasing its potential to build and manage sophisticated serverless applications on Kubernetes. By expanding upon the foundational knowledge of Knative's core componentsServices, Routes, Revisions, and Configurations — we explored how these elements interact to address complex use cases. By integrating the advanced features discussed in this chapter, you are now equipped to handle increasingly complex serverless challenges, paving the way for highly optimized, scalable, and future-proof applications.

- **Advanced Traffic Management:** Knative's pluggable architecture and integration with ingress solutions such as Istio, Kourier, and Gloo enable precise traffic routing, contextual decision-making, and advanced deployment strategies like canary releases and A/B testing.

- **Service Mesh Synergy:** By integrating Knative with service meshes, we unlock powerful capabilities such as mutual TLS, enhanced observability, and robust traffic control, ensuring greater security and scalability for serverless applications.

- **Performance Monitoring and Optimization:** Leveraging tools like Prometheus, Grafana, and Jaeger alongside Knative's native metrics equips you to maintain optimal resource utilization, troubleshoot bottlenecks, and ensure your applications are performant and cost-effective.

- **Dynamic Deployment Management:** The seamless interplay between Revisions, Routes, and Configurations enables efficient version control, rollback strategies, and continuous deployment workflows, allowing teams to adapt swiftly to changing requirements.

Knative Serving exemplifies the potential of cloud-native, serverless platforms to simplify operations, enhance scalability, and improve resilience. By mastering these advanced capabilities, you are now equipped to deploy, secure, and scale serverless applications with greater confidence. But there is one more crucial piece to the puzzle — Auto-scaling.

Looking Ahead: In the next chapter, we will dive into Auto-scaling a cornerstone of serverless computing. We will explore how Knative leverages advanced scaling mechanisms, such as scale-to-zero and custom metric-based scaling, to dynamically adjust resource allocation and optimize application responsiveness. These techniques ensure that your applications remain responsive, cost-efficient, and resilient under varying workloads.

6

Auto-Scaling

> ...What works at scale
> may be different from
> scaling what works. Pilots
> often succeed, while
> scale-up often fails when
> the context changes.
>
> *(Rohini Nilekani)*

What happens when your e-commerce platform suddenly experiences 10x more traffic during a flash sale? How do you prevent slowdowns and crashes without over-provisioning expensive infrastructure? Can your application scale down to zero when idle, cutting costs without sacrificing availability? In traditional models of service delivery, scaling to meet demand has always been a double-edged sword. On one side, the ability to scale up resources ensures that applications can handle increases in traffic without degradation in performance. On the other, it introduces a set of challenges and complexities that organizations must navigate. Provisioning for peak demand often means purchasing and maintaining excess capacity that sits idle most of the time, leading to inefficiencies and inflated costs. Moreover, the manual intervention required to scale resources in response to traffic patterns introduces latency in response times and potential for human error, not to mention the operational overhead of monitoring and managing this scaling process. This latency in provisioning capacity means that application responsiveness is perpetually playing catch-up with the increase in traffic.

Auto-scaling is a cornerstone feature of serverless architectures, allowing applications to efficiently handle varying loads by automatically adjusting the number of running instances.This dynamic scalingextending to accommodate traffic spikes and retracting into quiescence when idleis what makes the serverless model both powerful and cost-effective. With Knative, applications automatically scale up in response to traffic surges, ensuring availability and performance, and just as importantly, scale down to zero when idle, optimizing resource use and minimizing costs. This elasticity is managed by the platform, relieving developers and operations teams from the burdens of capacity planning and manual scaling.

This shift from manual to automated resource optimization underlines the serverless promise: to enhance efficiency, reduce operational costs, and freeing developers to focus on innovation rather than operational concerns. It also marks a pivotal advancement in how we manage and scale our applications. In this chapter, we will explore Knative's auto-scaling features focusing on how to configure and leverage these capabilities to meet real-world operational demands. To understand how Knative's auto-scaling achieves these benefits, we'll explore the following areas within this chapter:

- ▶ Understand the core principles of Knative Auto-Scaling.
- ▶ Explore how Knative scales services down to zero to optimize costs.
- ▶ Implement concurrency-based scaling to improve efficiency.
- ▶ Configure auto-scaling settings with hands-on practical examples.

6.1 Auto-Scaling Principles

Knative Serving dynamically manages the scaling of services, from serving a handful of requests to serving thousands of concurrent requests, and even downscaling services to zero instances when not in use. Knative's auto-scaling behavior is governed by observable metrics. By default, Knative Serving utilizes the number of in-flight concurrent requests to a service as the primary scaling metric. As the number of concurrent in-flight requests to a services increases, Knative spins up more containers to handle these requests. When the number of concurrent in-flight requests decreases, Knative destroys these additional containers and releases resources back. However, Knative allows for customization to base scaling decisions on other metrics like CPU utilization or custom metrics defined by the service.

When the observed scaling metric for a service exceeds a configured threshold, Knative initiates a scale-up process. This typically involves provisioning new pods (replicas) of the Service's container image to distribute the incoming load, ensuring your application remains responsive.

Note that pod creation and initialization are not instantaneous. This interval, along with potential networking setup time, should be factored into expectations of how quickly Knative responds to a surge. Factoring in these intervals helps set realistic expectations, especially for services that might experience sudden, unpredictable traffic spikes. Knative offers advanced features, such as the Knative Pod Autoscaler (KPA), to mitigate scaling delays by preemptively provisioning pods. We'll explore these techniques in more depth later in the chapter.

Conversely, when the scaling metric falls below a threshold for a sustained period, Knative initiates scale-down. Knative prioritizes a smooth user experience during scale-down. It doesn't abruptly terminate pods but provides them time to finish serving any existing requests before they are removed from service. This ensures active requests are completed before termination and removal.

If traffic ceases completely and sufficient time elapses (configurable), Knative will scale the service down to zero pods. This is a hallmark of serverless, optimizing resource usage. This optimizes resource usage and can potentially reduce costs in pay-per-use environments. Knative employs concepts like 'stable windows' and configurable timeouts to prevent unnecessary scaling churn due to temporary dips in traffic. This ensures that your application scales in a way that is both responsive to demand and efficient in its use of resources.

Knative provides various configuration options to fine-tune and set thresholds for scaling (e.g., the minimum and maximum number of pods). This flexibility empowers developers to tailor auto-scaling behavior to suit the specific workload and performance characteristics of their services. This behavior is governed by several configurable parameters, including:

- *Minimum and Maximum Scale*: Defines the lower and upper bounds for the number of instances.

- *Target Concurrency*: Specifies the desired number of concurrent requests each instance should handle, influencing how quickly Knative scales up or down.

Understanding these parameters is key to tuning your Knative services for optimal performance and resource utilization. We will look at these configuration parameters in section 6.6

6.2 Scaling Strategies and Configurations

Knative Serving offers flexibility in how you configure auto-scaling for your applications. Understanding these strategies and their associated configurations is crucial for optimizing performance and resource usage.

6.2.1 Request-Based Scaling

By default, Knative scales services based on the number of concurrent requests. Knative monitors incoming requests and adjusts the number of pods (instances) to handle the current load. This strategy suits web applications, APIs, and event-driven systems where responsiveness to incoming requests is vital. This enables the application to be responsive to changing traffic patterns and enables efficient resource utilization. This may lead to over-provisioning during sudden spikes and doesn't account for request complexity or resource intensity.

```
 1  apiVersion: serving.knative.dev/v1
 2  kind: Service
 3  metadata:
 4    name: example-service
 5  spec:
 6    template:
 7      spec:
 8        containers:
 9          - image: example/image
10    traffic:
11    - percent: 100
12      revisionName: example-service
```

```
13  autoscaling:
14    metric: concurrency
15    target: 100
16    minScale: 1
17    maxScale: 10
```

Listing 6.1: containerConcurrency Setting

In the above example, I am configuring a service named example-service and configure the following for autoscaling.

- **metric: concurrency**: This sets the auto-scaling metric to concurrent requests, meaning the service scales based on the number of active requests.

- **target: 100**: Each pod is configured to handle up to 100 concurrent requests.

- **minScale: 1**: This ensures that at least one pod is always running, maintaining availability.

- **maxScale: 10**: This limits the maximum number of pods to 10, preventing over-provisioning.

This configuration enables the service to scale dynamically based on incoming request load, making it ideal for web applications, APIs, and event-driven systems that require responsiveness. However, it's important to note that this strategy might lead to over-provisioning during sudden traffic spikes, as it does not account for the complexity or resource intensity of individual requests.

6.2.2 CPU-Based Scaling

For CPU-intensive applications, scaling based on CPU utilization can be more efficient. Knative allows configuring services to scale based on pod CPU usage, ensuring adequate resources for computationally demanding tasks. This strategy is ideal for Applications with predictable CPU usage patterns, CPU-intensive applications or background processing tasks. It ensures efficient resource utilization for CPU-bound tasks and reduces waste from over-provisioning. This strategy requires accurate CPU utilization monitoring and may not respond quickly to sudden traffic changes.

```
1  apiVersion: serving.knative.dev/v1
2  kind: Service
3  metadata:
4    name: example-service
5  spec:
6    template:
7      spec:
8        containers:
9        - image: example/image
10    traffic:
11    - percent: 100
12      revisionName: example-service
13    autoscaling:
14      metric: cpu
15      targetUtilization: 70
16      minScale: 1
17      maxScale: 10
18      threshold: 50m
```

Listing 6.2: containerConcurrency Setting

In the above example, for auto-scaling, we configure the following:

- **metric: cpu**: This sets the auto-scaling metric to CPU usage, meaning the service scales based on the pod's CPU utilization.

- **target: 70**: Each pod is configured to handle up to 70% CPU utilization.

- **minScale: 1**: Ensures that at least one pod is always running, maintaining availability.

- **maxScale: 10**: Limits the maximum number of pods to 10, preventing over-provisioning.

- **threshold: 50m**: This sets a threshold of 50 millicores for the CPU metric.

This configuration ensures that the service dynamically adjusts to handle CPU-intensive workloads effectively. It's particularly beneficial for applications with consistent CPU usage patterns or tasks that demand high computational power. However, it's crucial to have accurate CPU monitoring in place to ensure the scaling strategy responds efficiently to the workload, while also acknowledging that it may not react as swiftly to sudden traffic changes.

6.2.3 Custom Metrics-Based Scaling

Knative also supports scaling based on custom metrics. This provides flexibility for applications with unique scaling requirements, such as scaling based on queue length, response times, or other application-specific metrics. Knative integrates with external metrics systems (e.g., Prometheus) to monitor custom metrics and adjust scaling appropriately. This strategy is ideal for applications with unique scaling requirements. Some complex systems have multiple scaling factors or may depend on Business-logic-driven scaling. This strategy provides the flexibility to adapt to unique application needs. It accounts for external factors influencing scalability and allows for business-logic-driven scaling decisions.

```
1  apiVersion: serving.knative.dev/v1
2  kind: Service
3  metadata:
4    name: example-service
5  spec:
6    template:
7      spec:
8        containers:
9        - image: example/image
10   traffic:
11   - percent: 100
12     revisionName: example-service
13   autoscaling:
14     metric: external
15     external:
16       metricName: queue_length
17       namespace: default
18       selector:
19         matchLabels:
20           app: example
21     target: 10
22     minScale: 1
23     maxScale: 10
```

Listing 6.3: containerConcurrency Setting

6.3 Scaling to Zero

One of Knative's defining features is its ability to scale applications down to zero instances, essentially pausing services during periods of inactivity. Knative achieves scale-to-zero by dynamically removing all pods associated with a service after a period of inactivity. Essentially, if no requests are being made to the service, Knative eliminates its resource footprint entirely. Unlike traditional models where applications run continuously, consuming resources regardless of demand, scale-to-zero embodies the serverless promise of true operational efficiency. This paradigm shift not only optimizes cloud resource utilization but also paves the way for a more sustainable and cost-effective approach to application deployment. In environments where resource consumption directly correlates with costs, the ability to scale-to-zero transforms the economics of deploying services, ensuring you pay only for active computing time.

The scale-to-zero capability of Knative not only exemplifies operational efficiency and cost savings but also aligns with the principles of green computing. By dynamically scaling down unused services to zero, Knative contributes to a more sustainable use of computing resources, reducing the energy consumption and carbon footprint associated with maintaining idle infrastructure.

To allow Knative to scale your service down to zero, the containerConcurrency setting in your Knative configuration should generally be set to 0. Knative uses configurable idle timeouts to determine how long it waits after the last request before scaling down to zero. Adjusting this parameter allows you to fine-tune the balance between cost optimization and responsiveness.

6.4 Cold start

A cold start occurs when a serverless function is invoked after being idle, with no running instances to serve the request. In the context of Knative, this happens when a service scales down to zero instances due to inactivity. When a new request arrives after a service has scaled to zero, there will be a slight delay while a new pod is created and the application initializes. Aggressive scaling to zero maximizes cost savings. However, scale-to-zero functionality introduces considerations around latency due to cold startsthat occur when scaling up from zero instances. The most immediate impact of a cold start is increased latency for the first request after scaling to zero, potentially affecting user experience.

A significant factor influencing cold start latency is the size of the container image used by your Knative service. Large image files require more time to download from the container registry to the cluster node where the new pod will run. Optimizing your container images for size by minimizing dependencies and using multi-stage builds can significantly reduce cold start delays. Beyond image size, the time it takes for your application code to initialize within the container can also contribute to cold start delays. This includes any startup tasks or scripts that run when the container starts up. This includes loading libraries, starting frameworks, and any other bootstrapping operations. Identifying and streamlining these initialization processes can help minimize cold start latency. When a new pod is created, there's a period of network setup involved. This includes establishing connections with services like databases or message queues. While typically brief, this network overhead can add to the overall cold start delay, especially if your application relies heavily on external resources.

Optimizing for minimal cold start latency involves careful configuration of scaling parameters and potentially pre-warming instances for highly responsive applications. Keeping instances warm with a slightly longer idle timeout can improve the speed of the first request after inactivity. Building container images with minimal dependencies and utilizing multi-stage builds significantly reduces their size, leading to faster download times during cold starts. Streamlining your application code's startup logic can minimize initialization times within the container. This might involve optimizing resource loading or deferring non-critical tasks until after the initial request is served.

While optimizing for cold starts, it's essential to navigate the trade-off between responsiveness and resource efficiency. Striking a balance requires understanding the specific demands of your application and its typical traffic patterns. For services where instant responsiveness is paramount, maintaining a minimal number of running instances may be justified. Conversely, for less critical services, embracing the scale-to-zero model more aggressively can lead to significant resource savings.

6.5 Concurrency-based Scaling

Concurrency refers to the number of requests that a single service instance can handle simultaneously. Unlike traditional scaling metrics that might focus solely on the number of incoming requests or CPU/memory utilization, concurrency-based scaling allows for more nuanced control over application performance and resource allocation. This approach aligns with the event-driven, stateless nature of serverless computing, where managing the flow of concurrent requests efficiently is paramount.

Knative Serving introduces concurrency as a first-class metric for auto-scaling. It allows developers to specify the desired level of concurrent requests a single pod can handle. When this threshold is exceeded, Knative triggers the creation of new pods to distribute the load, ensuring that each instance maintains optimal performance according to the defined concurrency levels. This focus on concurrency aligns well with applications that experience fluctuating workloads.

Knative allows you to configure thresholds related to the number of concurrent requests. Imagine you set a concurrency threshold of 10. If the number of in-flight requests surpasses 10 for a sustained period, Knative initiates a scale-up process, provisioning new pods (containers) to distribute the load and maintain performance. Conversely, when the number of concurrent requests falls below a defined threshold for a set amount of time, Knative scales down, gracefully terminating pods to optimize resource utilization. This approach is particularly effective for applications that handle a burst of short-lived tasks, such as web servers or API gateways.

Implementing concurrency-based scaling involves trade-offs between throughput, latency, and resource efficiency. Higher concurrency levels can increase resource utilization but may lead to decreased performance per request. Conversely, lower concurrency targets might improve individual request handling but underutilize available resources. The key is to find a balance that meets your application's performance goals while optimizing for cost and efficiency.

While concurrency-based scaling excels in many scenarios, it's important to consider its limitations. This approach might not be ideal for applications with long-running tasks or those with high CPU or memory demands. In such cases, scaling based on CPU usage, memory usage, or custom metrics might be more appropriate.

6.6 Hands-on Auto-Scaling Configuration

Knative Serving offers several key parameters for configuring auto-scaling behavior. Understanding these parameters is crucial for customizing how your services scale:

- Container Concurrency (containerConcurrency): Specifies the maximum number of requests that can be processed simultaneously by a single instance of the service. This setting directly influences concurrency-based scaling.
- Scaling Window (stable-window): Defines the time window used to evaluate service metrics for scaling decisions. A longer window smooths out short-term fluctuations in traffic, whereas a shorter window allows for more responsive scaling.

➤ Minimum and Maximum Scale (minScale and maxScale): Determines the minimum and maximum number of instances that your service can scale to. minScale can be used to keep a certain number of instances running to avoid cold starts.

6.6.1 Adjusting Container Concurrency

To modify the container concurrency for your service, update the containerConcurrency field in your service configuration:

```
apiVersion: serving.knative.dev/v1
kind: Service
metadata:
  name: example-service
spec:
  template:
    spec:
      containerConcurrency: 5
      containers:
      - image: gcr.io/my-project/my-application
```

Listing 6.4: containerConcurrency Setting

6.6.2 Configuring the Scaling Window

To adjust the scaling window, you'll need to modify the auto-scaling.knative.dev/stable-window annotation in your service configuration:

```
metadata:
  annotations:
    autoscaling.knative.dev/stable-window: 60s
```

Listing 6.5: autoscaling Setting

6.6.3 Setting Min and Max Scale

To ensure that your service always has a minimum number of instances running, or to limit the maximum number of instances, configure minScale and maxScale annotations:

```
metadata:
  annotations:
    autoscaling.knative.dev/minScale: 1
    autoscaling.knative.dev/maxScale: 10
```

Listing 6.6: min/max Setting

After applying your configurations, monitor your service's scaling behavior under various traffic conditions. Knative provides metrics and logs that can help you understand how your service responds to different settings, allowing you to fine-tune your configurations for optimal performance and resource usage. By understanding and customizing autoscaling parameters, you can ensure that your serverless applications are both responsive to user demand and efficient in resource usage.

6.7 Configuring auto-scaling

To demonstrate the practical application of Knative's auto-scaling capabilities, let's configure the auto-scaling parameters for our e-commerce application. This involves editing the service's YAML definition to include auto-scaling annotations that specify our desired scaling behavior.

For example, to set a minimum of 1 instance and a maximum of 10 instances, with a target of 50 concurrent requests per instance, we'd add the following annotations to our Knative Service:

```
1   apiVersion: serving.knative.dev/v1
2   kind: Service
3   metadata:
4     name: dotnet-example-service
5     annotations:
6       autoscaling.knative.dev/minScale: 1  # Always keep at
      least 1 pod running
7       autoscaling.knative.dev/maxScale: 10 # Limit scaling to a
      maximum of 10 pods
8       autoscaling.knative.dev/target: 50 # target of 50
      concurrent requests per instance
```

Listing 6.7: min/max Setting

6.8 Summary

In this chapter, we explored Knative's auto-scaling capabilities — a cornerstone of serverless architectures. You learned how Knative seamlessly scales your application's services up and down in response to demand, ensuring optimal performance and resource efficiency.

Key takeaways from this chapter include:

- ➽ Understanding Auto-Scaling Principles: We delved into the core principles behind Knative's auto-scaling. You learned about the role of metrics (like concurrent requests), scaling thresholds, and how Knative intelligently provisions or removes pods to match the workload.
- ➽ Scale-to-Zero: We explored one of Knative's defining features, its ability to scale services down to zero instances. This functionality not only conserves resources but also aligns with the pay-for-what-you-use model, making serverless architectures financially and sustainably attractive.

- Cold Start: An important consideration in serverless scaling, we covered strategies for mitigating cold start latency, ensuring that services remain responsive even as they scale from zero.
- Concurrency-Based Scaling: We explained Knative's default reliance on concurrent requests as a scaling metric, highlighting its natural alignment with e-commerce workloads. You learned how to configure parameters like `containerConcurrency` to influence scaling behavior.
- Hands-On Configuration: Through practical examples, including adjustments to our e-commerce sample application, we demonstrated how to configure and optimize Knative's auto-scaling parameters. This hands-on section provided insights into tailoring auto-scaling behavior to meet the specific needs of different services within an application.

6.8.1 Moving Forward

While auto-scaling ensures your application dynamically adapts to traffic patterns, modern applications require more than just scalingthey need to be event-driven. In the real world, applications must react in real-time to triggers such as user actions, system events, and external APIs.

In the next part, **Event-Driven Architectures and Knative Eventing**, we will explore how to build reactive systems that respond to events in real time. You'll learn how Knative Eventing enables seamless event routing, orchestration, and integration across diverse services and systems.

As we dive into Part 3, we'll move beyond scaling individual services to designing workflows and patterns that empower your application to act, react, and scale in response to dynamic events. With Knative Eventing, you'll unlock the potential to build resilient, decoupled, and event-driven systems that are truly serverless at their core. Let's continue the journey into event-driven serverless architectures!

Part III

Event-Driven Architectures and Knative Eventing

7

Event-Driven Architecture Fundamentals

> ... The master has failed
> more times than the
> beginner has even tried.
>
> *(Stephen McCranie)*

Welcome to Part 3 of our journey into serverless computing with Knative. In Part 2, we explored Knative Serving and learned how it simplifies the deployment, scaling, and management of serverless applications. Now, we turn our focus to the dynamic world of event-driven architectures

(EDA) and Knative Eventing, which empower serverless components to communicate and react to real-time events efficiently.

In the previous chapters, we explored how Knative Serving simplifies the design, deployment, and management of serverless applications. However, serverless applications are not isolated entities; they need to interact seamlessly with other services, trigger actions, and respond dynamically to real-world events. Unlike traditional applications that rely on constant polling or synchronous request-response cycles, serverless functions are ephemeral — they run only when triggered and scale down when idle. In such environments, event-driven communication is the backbone that enables stateless, scalable, and cost-efficient architectures. This is where Knative Eventing comes into play, enabling these serverless components to communicate through events and react asynchronously to changes and actions. Before diving into the specifics of Knative Eventing, it's crucial to understand the underlying principles of event-driven architectures.

Traditional architectures struggle with scalability, cost efficiency, and real-time responsiveness — especially in serverless environments where functions are ephemeral and scale dynamically. Event-driven architectures (EDA) solve these challenges by ensuring that serverless functions are executed only when necessary, enabling asynchronous, loosely coupled interactions between microservices. This reactive approach is critical for modern cloud-native applications, as it allows them to efficiently handle spikes in demand, real-time data processing, and inter-service communication without manual scaling or persistent infrastructure. In this chapter, we'll explore the principles of EDA and its crucial role in serverless computing, setting the stage for understanding how Knative Eventing seamlessly enables event-driven workflows on Kubernetes.

In this chapter, we will cover:

- Understanding Event-Driven Architectures
- Event-Driven Architecture Patterns
- Challenges and Pitfalls of Event-Driven Architectures
- Building Event-Driven Applications
- Performance at Scale

7.1 EDA - The Serverless Advantage

Serverless architectures offer dynamic scaling and pay-per-execution model, making them highly efficient. However, traditional synchronous request-response models can undermine this efficiency, leading to wasted compute resources due to idle instances, latency and bottlenecks from inefficient scaling under unpredictable loads, and complex inter-service communication challenges, including manual retries, failures, and synchronization issues. By contrast, EDA enables serverless functions to operate in a reactive, event-triggered manner, eliminating idle compute time, optimizing resource consumption, and promoting scalability, resilience, and agility. Serverless computing and Event-Driven Architecture (EDA) have a synergistic relationship. The on-demand, stateless nature of serverless functions aligns perfectly with the asynchronous, event-driven communication model. Let's explore how EDA enhances serverless computing in key areas:

7.1.1 Efficiency and Cost Optimization

- **Reduced Idle Time**: EDA complements serverless by ensuring functions are triggered only when specific events occur, eliminating idle compute time and dramatically reducing costs.

- **Pay-per-Use Alignment**: The event-driven nature of EDA aligns with the pay-per-use model of serverless, as functions are invoked and scaled in direct response to event occurrences, optimizing resource consumption and cost efficiency.

7.1.2 Scalability and Resilience

- **Independent Scaling**: EDA enables serverless functions to scale independently based on the volume of their triggering events. This granular scaling allows the system to adapt dynamically to varying workloads without over-provisioning resources.

- **Fault Isolation**: The decoupled nature of EDA promotes fault isolation in serverless applications. If one function fails, it doesn't directly impact others, enhancing the overall resilience of the system.

7.1.3 Development Agility

- **Simplified Development**: EDA simplifies the development of serverless applications by allowing developers to focus on writing individual functions that respond to specific events. This modularity promotes code reusability and maintainability.

- **Faster Iteration**: The decoupled nature of EDA enables faster iteration cycles in serverless development. Developers can update or add new functions without affecting other parts of the system, promoting agility and rapid innovation.

By understanding and leveraging the synergy between serverless and EDA, developers can unlock the full potential of both paradigms to build modern, cloud-native applications that are scalable, resilient, and cost-efficient.

7.2 Event-Driven Architectures

Event-Driven Architecture (EDA) is a software design pattern where applications are triggered by events — occurrences or changes in state that are significant to the system. These events can originate from user actions (like clicking a button), sensor readings, system notifications, or even changes in data within your application. At the core of serverless scalability is the ability to react dynamically to changing workloads. Event-Driven Architecture (EDA) enables this by decoupling services, allowing them to execute only when needed — instead of relying on a continuous polling or request-response cycle. Instead, services in an EDA communicate asynchronously by producing and consuming these events. This decoupled approach makes systems more flexible, scalable, and resilient.

Serverless computing is built on on-demand execution — functions and workloads only run when triggered and scale down when idle. Unlike monolithic or microservice-based architectures that use constant polling or always-running processes, serverless applications must be event-driven to function efficiently. Event-driven architecture (EDA) is a key enabler of the power and efficiency of serverless computing. By triggering functions only when specific events occur, EDA eliminates idle compute, ensuring resources are used only when needed and dramatically reducing costs. The asynchronous nature of EDA allows serverless functions to remain lightweight and stateless, focusing solely on business logic while externalizing state management. This decoupling inherent in EDA further empowers dynamic scaling, as serverless platforms can independently scale individual functions based on the volume of their triggering events. Ultimately, EDA provides the architectural foundation that allows serverless components to operate independently, evolve more easily, and scale efficiently, maximizing the benefits of this cloud-native paradigm.

In comparison to traditional request-response architectures, EDA offers significant benefits, especially in terms of scalability, resilience, and agility. Let's look at some of the benefits of EDA.

- **Decoupling**: Services operate independently without needing to know the details of other services. This makes it easier to develop, test, and scale induvidual services independently. Example: In an e-commerce platform, the order service doesn't need to know about the inventory service. When an order is placed, it simply emits an order placed event. The inventory service listens for this event and updates stock levels accordingly.

- **Scalability**: Services can scale independently based on workload. Example: A notification service can scale up during peak times (like promotional events) to handle increased messaging loads without affecting other services like payment processing.

- **Resilience**: By breaking systems into loosely coupled components, faults can be isolated. This prevents cascading failures and improves the overall resilience of the system. Example: If the shipping service goes down, it doesn't prevent orders from being placed. Once it recovers, it can process any pending order placed events.

To fully leverage these advantages, it is essential to understand the key components that form the backbone of an event-driven architecture and how they interact to create a loosely coupled, scalable system.

7.2.1 Key Components and Event Flow in EDA

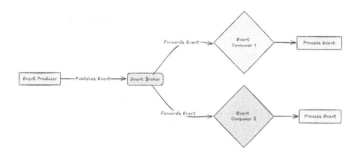

Figure 7.1: Key Components and Event Flow in EDA

As shown in Figure 7.1, you can see the key players in an EDA:

- **Event Producer**: This could be anything that generates an event, such as a user interacting with a website, a sensor detecting a change, or a service completing a task.

- **Event Broker**: This is the intermediary that receives events from producers and routes them to the appropriate consumers. It acts as a central hub for event distribution.

- **Event Consumers**: These are the applications or services that react to the events. They might perform actions, update data, or trigger further events in response.

For example, in an e-commerce application, when a customer places an order (the event), an order service publishes an order placed event to the broker. An inventory service (consumer) might react to this event by updating stock levels, while a notification service (another consumer) might send an email confirmation to the customer. These services are decoupled; they don't need to know about each other directly, only about the events they care about.

7.2.2 Event Producers, Consumers, and Brokers

Let's take a closer look at the roles and responsibilities of these key components:

Event Producers

Definition: Event producers are the sources that initiate events within an event-driven system. They are responsible for detecting or recognizing that something significant has occurred and then generating an event to represent that occurrence.

Responsibilities:

- **Event Detection:** Producers must be able to identify when an event of interest happens. This could involve monitoring user actions, system changes, data updates, or external triggers.

- **Event Creation:** Producers create the event message, which includes information about what happened, when it happened, and any relevant data associated with the event.

- **Event Publishing:** Producers send the event message to an event broker or messaging system for distribution.

Examples:

- A web application that generates an event when a user submits a form.

- An IoT sensor that publishes an event when it detects a change in temperature.

- A microservice that emits an event when it completes a task.

Event Consumers

Definition: Event consumers are the applications or services that receive and react to events. They are responsible for processing events and taking appropriate actions based on the information they contain.

Responsibilities:

- **Event Subscription:** Consumers subscribe to specific types of events or topics they are interested in.

- **Event Reception:** Consumers receive events from the event broker or messaging system.

- **Event Processing:** Consumers process the received events, which might involve updating databases, triggering other services, or performing calculations.

Examples:

- A notification service that sends an email to a user when a new account is created (reacting to an account created event).

- A payment processing service that initiates a transaction when an order is placed (reacting to an order placed event).

- An analytics service that aggregates data based on events received from various sources.

Event Brokers

Definition: Event brokers are intermediary components that manage the routing and delivery of events between producers and consumers. They act as a central hub for event distribution, decoupling producers from consumers.

Responsibilities:

- **Event Reception:** Brokers receive events from producers.

- **Event Storage (Optional):** Some brokers store events temporarily or persistently to provide durability and ensure delivery even if consumers are unavailable.

- **Event Routing:** Brokers route events to the appropriate consumers based on subscriptions or routing rules.

- **Delivery Guarantees:** Brokers often provide different levels of delivery guarantees, such as at least once or exactly once delivery.

Examples:

- Apache Kafka: A high-throughput, distributed streaming platform.

- RabbitMQ: A versatile message broker that supports various messaging patterns.

- Amazon SNS/SQS: Cloud-based messaging services provided by AWS.

To illustrate these interactions further, consider a ride-hailing application. When a user requests a ride (the event), the 'rider app' (event producer) publishes a 'ride requested' event to the broker (e.g., Kafka).

A 'driver app' (event consumer) subscribed to this event type receives the request and displays it to nearby drivers. When a driver accepts the ride, the 'driver app' publishes a 'ride accepted' event, which the 'rider app' consumes to update the user's screen. The broker manages the flow of these events between the different components.

Component	Responsibilities	Examples
Event Producers	<ul><li>Detect events</li><li>Create event messages</li><li>Publish events to brokers</li></ul>	<ul><li>User interface actions</li><li>IoT sensors</li><li>Microservices</li></ul>
Event Consumers	<ul><li>Subscribe to events</li><li>Receive and process events</li><li>Perform actions based on event data</li></ul>	<ul><li>Notification services</li><li>Payment processors</li><li>Analytics</li></ul>
Event Brokers	<ul><li>Receive events from producers</li><li>Store events (optional)</li><li>Route events to consumers</li><li>Ensure delivery</li></ul>	<ul><li>Apache Kafka</li><li>RabbitMQ</li><li>AWS SNS/SQS</li></ul>

Table 7.1: Components, Responsibilities, and Examples in Event-Driven Systems

7.3 Event-Driven Architecture Patterns

In the world of event-driven architecture, one size doesn't fit all. Just like an architect chooses different structural patterns for building a skyscraper versus a bridge, software architects need to select the right EDA patterns to create robust and efficient systems. These patterns provide established solutions to common challenges in event-driven systems, helping you design applications that are scalable, maintainable, and resilient.

Choosing the right EDA pattern can significantly impact your application's performance, its ability to handle growing event volumes, and how easily you can make changes in the future. By understanding the strengths and weaknesses of different patterns, you can make informed decisions that align with your specific needs.

While there are numerous EDA patterns, we'll focus on the most common and relevant ones for building serverless applications with Knative: Publish-Subscribe, Event Sourcing, and CQRS (Command Query Responsibility Segregation). These patterns provide a solid foundation for designing event-driven systems and are particularly well-suited for the serverless paradigm.

7.3.1 Pub/Sub Pattern

The **Publish-Subscribe (Pub/Sub)** pattern is a foundational pattern. In this pattern, **Producers** publish events to a specific topic or channel on an event broker. **Consumers** subscribe to topics they're interested in and receive only the events relevant to them.

This decoupling between producers and consumers offers several advantages:

- **Loose Coupling:** Producers and consumers are independent. Producers don't need to know who's listening, and consumers don't need to know who's sending events.

- **Scalability:** Multiple consumers can subscribe to the same topic, allowing for easy scaling to handle a large number of event recipients.

- **Flexibility:** New consumers can be added at any time without affecting existing producers or consumers.

Pub/Sub is particularly well-suited for scenarios like:

- **Real-time Notifications:** Sending alerts, updates, or notifications to users (e.g., new messages in a chat application, stock price changes).

- **Event Broadcasting:** Distributing events to a large number of recipients (e.g., social media feeds, news updates).

- **Asynchronous Workflows:** Triggering background processes or tasks in response to events (e.g., processing orders, generating reports).

In serverless architectures, the Publish-Subscribe (Pub/Sub) pattern is fundamental for decoupling microservices. Instead of services calling each other directly, Pub/Sub allows producers to publish events to a central Broker, while consumers scale dynamically based on demand.

7.3.2 Event Sourcing

Event Sourcing takes a different approach to managing application state. Instead of storing only the current state of an object, Event Sourcing records every change to that object as a sequence of events. Think of it like a detailed logbook that captures every action taken on an object throughout its lifecycle.

Here's how it works:

1. An event representing a change to the object's state is generated (e.g., `OrderCreated`, `OrderUpdated`, `OrderShipped`).

2. This event is appended to an immutable event log.

3. The application state is derived by replaying the events in the log.

Benefits of Event Sourcing:

- **Complete Audit Trail:** Provides a comprehensive history of all changes, making it easy to track how an object reached its current state.

- **Temporal Queries:** Allows you to reconstruct the state of an object at any point in time.

- **Debugging and Auditing:** Facilitates debugging by traveling back in time to see the sequence of events leading to an issue.

However, Event Sourcing also introduces complexities:

- **Storage:** Storing a potentially large number of events can require significant storage capacity.

- **Querying:** Querying the current state requires replaying events, which can be less efficient than directly accessing the latest state.

- **Schema Evolution:** Changing the structure of events over time requires careful handling to maintain compatibility with past events.

7.3.3 Command Query Responsibility Segregation

CQRS (Command Query Responsibility Segregation) is a pattern that separates read and write operations for a data store. It addresses the challenges of having different performance and scalability requirements for reading and writing data.

In CQRS:

- **Commands:** Represent actions that change the application state (e.g., creating a new user, placing an order).

- **Queries:** Represent requests for retrieving data without modifying the state (e.g., getting user details, searching for products).

By separating commands and queries, you can optimize each operation independently. For example, you might use a highly scalable database for handling write operations and a separate, read-optimized database for handling queries.

CQRS often works well with Event Sourcing. Commands can generate events that are then used to update the write database and are stored in the event log. The read database can be populated by replaying events from the event log.

Benefits of CQRS:

- **Improved Performance:** Allows for specialized data stores and optimized query mechanisms.

- **Increased Scalability:** Enables independent scaling of read and write operations.

- **Simplified Development:** Separates concerns and simplifies the development of read and write logic.

However, CQRS adds complexity to the system, requiring careful consideration of data synchronization and consistency between the read and write models.

7.3.4 Choosing the Right Pattern

Selecting the appropriate event-driven pattern depends on the specific needs of your application. When selecting an architecture pattern, it's essential to evaluate factors such as scalability requirements, data consistency needs, and the complexity of your system.

- **Scalability Requirements**: When considering scalability needs, it's essential to ask how many events you expect to handle, whether you need to support a large number of consumers, and if your event volume will grow significantly over time. If scalability is a primary concern, Pub/Sub should be a strong contender due to its ability to handle high event volumes and support numerous consumers.

- **Consistency Requirements**: When evaluating data consistency requirements, consider how critical it is to maintain strong consistency across your application, whether you need a complete audit trail of changes, and if you're working with sensitive data that requires strict consistency guarantees. If strong consistency and auditability are paramount, Event Sourcing offers a robust solution by recording every state change as an immutable event.

- **Complexity**: When considering application complexity, think about the level of complexity you're comfortable with and whether the benefits of a more complex pattern outweigh the added development and maintenance overhead. Event Sourcing and CQRS introduce complexity, so choose them only if their benefits — such as auditability and performance optimization — are essential for your application

Having explored the foundational patterns of event-driven architectures — including Publish-Subscribe, Event Sourcing, and CQRS — we can appreciate how these patterns offer robust solutions for building scalable, maintainable, and resilient systems. However, the effectiveness of these patterns in real-world applications hinges on their ability to perform under load and scale to meet growing demands. As organizations adopt these patterns, they often encounter challenges related to event volume, latency, and system resource utilization. To ensure your event-driven applications remain responsive and efficient, it's crucial to consider scalability and performance from the outset. In the next section, we'll dive into key strategies and best practices for scaling event-driven systems and optimizing their performance, enabling you to build applications that not only function well but also excel under pressure.

7.4 Performance at Scale

Scalability and performance are paramount in event-driven architectures, especially as systems grow and the volume of events increases. Without proper planning and implementation, systems can become bottlenecked, leading to high latency, message loss, or even system failure. In this section, we'll explore key strategies and best practices to ensure your event-driven systems can handle increasing demands efficiently and reliably.

7.4.1 Load Balancing Between Consumers

Imagine a highway with multiple lanes. Distributing traffic across these lanes ensures smoother flow and prevents congestion. Similarly, in an event-driven system, distributing the workload across multiple consumers prevents any single consumer from becoming a bottleneck. This is crucial for handling high event volumes and ensuring that your system can scale effectively. Load balancing ensures that the processing workload is evenly distributed among multiple consumer instances. In systems like Apache Kafka, consumers can be organized into consumer groups, where each consumer in the group processes a subset of the partitions. This mechanism allows for parallel processing while ensuring that each event is only processed once by the group. Additionally, implementing load balancers or leveraging broker features can help distribute events effectively and prevent any single consumer from becoming a bottleneck. This helps to meet increased demand while ensuring fault tolerance.

7.4.2 Horizontal Scaling for Brokers and Consumers

Just as you might widen a highway to accommodate more traffic, scaling your event infrastructure is essential for handling increased event volume. This includes scaling both your event brokers and your consumers. Horizontal scaling involves adding more instances of brokers or consumers to handle increased load, rather than adding more resources to existing instances (vertical scaling). This approach enhances fault tolerance and provides better scalability. Scaling your brokers ensures reliable event delivery even under heavy load. Scaling your consumers allows them to keep up with the rate of event production and prevent backpressure, where consumers are overwhelmed by the influx of events.

7.4.3 Handling High Throughput Scenarios

In high throughput scenarios, it's essential to optimize both the producers and consumers. Techniques like batching allow consumers to process multiple events together, reducing overhead per event. Buffering helps smooth out spikes in event rates by temporarily storing events before processing.

- **Buffering**: Temporarily store events in a buffer to handle bursts of incoming events and provide a more consistent flow to consumers.

- **Batching**: Group events together into batches to reduce the overhead of processing individual events.

- **Caching**: Store frequently accessed data in a cache to reduce latency and improve response times.

Tuning broker configurations, such as increasing the number of partitions in Kafka, can also enhance parallel processing capabilities and improve throughput. Using efficient serialization formats like Protocol Buffers or Avro can reduce message sizes and speed up serialization/deserialization.

7.4.4 Ensuring Message Ordering

In some applications, maintaining the order of events is crucial. Ordering is critical in scenarios such as financial transactions or inventory updates where the order of operations is important. Sequencing techniques can be used to ensure the order of events is maintained where necessary. Strategies like using a single consumer, message sequencing, or event sourcing can help ensure message ordering.

- **Single Consumer**: Process all events related to a specific entity (e.g., an order) with a single consumer to guarantee sequential processing.

- **Message Sequencing**: Assign sequence numbers to events to enforce ordering during processing.

- **Event Sourcing**: The inherent ordering of events in an event log can be used to ensure correct sequencing.

Choosing the appropriate strategy depends on your application's specific needs and the level of ordering required. While scaling strategies help event-driven systems perform efficiently, effective event design is just as crucial to ensure clarity, maintainability, and system interoperability. In the next section, we'll explore best practices for designing events that enhance the performance and scalability of your event-driven applications.

7.5 Event Design Best Practices

Addressing scalability and performance is vital for any event-driven architecture, but achieving optimal results goes beyond infrastructure and system tuning. The design of the events themselves plays a pivotal role in the overall efficiency and effectiveness of your system. Poorly designed events can lead to increased latency, unnecessary processing overhead, and difficulties in scaling your applications.

To build high-performing, scalable event-driven systems, it's essential to apply thoughtful event design principles. By adhering to best practices in event creation, naming conventions, payload structuring, and schema evolution, you can enhance the clarity, maintainability, and interoperability of your events. Lets explore some best practices to design events that contribute positively to your system's performance and scalability.

- **Event Granularity**: Determine the right level of detail for your events. Avoid making events too coarse or too fine-grained. Events should provide meaningful information that is not overwhelming. Too much detail can lead to large event payloads, while too little can make events less informative.

- **Idempotency**: Ensure your event handlers are idempotent, meaning they can be executed multiple times without causing unintended side effects. This is important for handling message redelivery scenarios. To achieve idempotency, you can use unique identifiers for each event and track processed events. This allows your consumers to recognize and ignore duplicate events, preventing errors and inconsistencies.

- **Schema Evolution**: As your application evolves, you might need to add new information to your events or change their structure. However, abruptly changing the format of an event can break existing consumers who are expecting the old format. Plan for schema evolution by using techniques that maintain compatibility with older consumers. This might involve versioning your events, adding optional fields, or providing default values for new fields.

By carefully managing schema changes, you can ensure that your event-driven system remains robust and adaptable as your application grows and evolves.

7.6   Challenges and Pitfalls of EDA

While event-driven architectures offer significant advantages, they also present unique challenges that require careful consideration. Building distributed systems with asynchronous communication can introduce complexities related to data consistency, debugging, error handling, and more. This section explores some of the common pitfalls and challenges you might encounter when working with EDA, along with strategies to address them effectively.

7.6.1   Eventual Consistency and Complexity

In a traditional system, when you update data, the changes are usually reflected immediately. However, in an event-driven system, services are decoupled and data updates might not be reflected instantly across all services. Eventual consistency arises because events are processed asynchronously. It might take some time for an event to propagate through the system and for all related services to update their state accordingly. It may take time for the entire system to become consistent and thus event-driven systems often exhibit eventual consistency. Managing data synchronization and consistency across decoupled services can be challenging. Implementing mechanisms to ensure consistency across services requires careful design and planning.

7.6.2 Debugging and Troubleshooting

Debugging distributed systems can be inherently challenging, as tracing event flows and identifying the root cause of issues can be difficult. Specialized tools and strategies are often required for effective debugging in event-driven architectures. Tools like **Jaeger** or **Zipkin** can help visualize event flows. Solutions like **ELK Stack** or **Fluentd** can help collect and correlate logs from multiple services.

7.6.3 Backpressure and Consumer Lag

When event consumers cannot keep up with the rate of events produced, it can lead to **backpressure** on the producers or consumer lag. Techniques like **rate limiting**, **buffering**, and **scaling consumers** can help manage backpressure and consumer lag. Monitoring consumer lag can also help identify bottlenecks early.

7.6.4 Handling Failure Scenarios

Event-driven systems can have multiple points of failure, including message delivery failures, consumer errors, and broker outages. Implementing error handling strategies such as retry mechanisms for transient failures, and dead-letter queues for events that cannot be processed is crucial for ensuring system resilience.

7.6.5 Monitoring and Observability

Monitoring and observability are essential for understanding the behavior of event-driven systems and identifying potential issues. Tools and techniques for tracking events, identifying bottlenecks, and troubleshooting problems are crucial. Knative integrates with various observability tools, making it easier to monitor and gain insights into your event-driven applications. Knative can integrate with tools like **Prometheus**, **Grafana**, and **Jaeger** to track events, identify bottlenecks, and troubleshoot issues.

These challenges highlight the importance of a robust eventing framework — one that simplifies event handling, observability, and resilience. By leveraging Knative Eventing, you can streamline the development of event-driven applications, enhance scalability, and improve fault tolerance, all while maintaining the benefits of serverless computing.

7.7 Building Event-Driven Applications

To build robust event-driven applications, it is essential to ensure that events are structured effectively and failures are managed gracefully. The first step in this process is designing event schemas that are clear, extensible, and maintainable over time.

7.7.1 Designing Event Schemas

Design your event payloads for clarity, consistency, and extensibility. This enables them to be clear, easy to understand, and evolve over time. Use versioning strategies to ensure new fields can be added without breaking existing consumers. Follow best practices for versioning and compatibility to ensure smooth schema evolution.

7.7.2 Handling Failures

Design your systems to handle failures gracefully, preventing cascading errors and ensuring data integrity. Implement retries for transient errors with exponential backoff to avoid overwhelming the system. When an event consistently fails, move it to a dead-letter queue for further analysis and to prevent data loss.

- **Retry Mechanisms**: Implement retry mechanisms to handle transient failures, such as temporary network issues or service unavailability. We will explore retry strategies in more detail in Chapter 8 and Chapter 9.

- **Dead-Letter Queues**: Use dead-letter queues to isolate and store problematic events that could not be delivered successfully, allowing for later analysis and potential recovery. We will explore DLQs in more depth in Section 8.7.1 of Chapter 8.

- **Compensating Actions**: Implement compensating actions to ensure data integrity in case of partial failures. Compensating actions can be used to undo operations that were performed based on an event that later turned out to be erroneous.

7.7.3 Knative Eventing and EDA

So far, we've explored the fundamentals of Event-Driven Architecture (EDA) and discussed its significant benefits for building serverless applications. We've seen how EDA enables decoupling, scalability, and resilience, which are crucial for maximizing the efficiency and cost-effectiveness of serverless architectures.

Knative Eventing provides a robust framework for building cloud native, event-driven applications on Kubernetes. It supports core event-driven concepts, including **Sources**, **Brokers**, and **Triggers**, simplifying the development and management of event-driven systems. Knative relies on **CloudEvents** to provide a standard way of describing events, ensuring interoperability between different systems. Design your event schemas to be compatible with CloudEvents, a specification for describing event data in a common way. This promotes interoperability and allows your applications to seamlessly integrate with other CloudEvents-compliant systems.

7.8 Summary

In this chapter, we explored the fundamentals of event-driven architectures (EDA) and their critical role in serverless computing. We examined how event producers, brokers, and consumers work together to create highly scalable, loosely coupled, and reactive systems — perfectly aligning with the on-demand execution model of serverless architectures.

Key takeaways from this chapter include:

- EDA and Serverless Synergy: How event-driven design enables efficient, cost-optimized serverless workloads by triggering execution only when needed.

- Core Components: Understanding the role of event producers, brokers, and consumers in an event-driven system.

- Architecture Patterns: Exploring Pub/Sub, Event Sourcing, and CQRS, and how they enhance scalability and fault tolerance in cloud-native applications.

- Challenges and Pitfalls: Addressing key concerns such as cold starts, observability, eventual consistency, and debugging asynchronous workflows.

In the next chapter, we'll see how these EDA fundamentals come to life within Kubernetes using **Knative Eventing** and explore how it leverages these principles to streamline the development of serverless, event-driven applications. While the principles in this chapter can be implemented with any messaging or broker system, Knative Eventing builds on these EDA principles, making them practical in Kubernetes-native serverless applications. By building on these core EDA concepts — Pub/Sub, Event Sourcing, CQRS — we'll discover how to configure event sources, route events via brokers and triggers, and standardize data with CloudEvents.

7.9 Next Steps

While EDA provides the foundation for scalable, event-driven applications, implementing it in a Kubernetes-based serverless environment requires the right tools and abstractions.

In the next chapter, we'll explore Knative Eventing — a powerful Kubernetes-native framework that enables seamless event routing, service orchestration, and dynamic scaling. You'll learn how Knative provides pre-built event sources, brokers, and triggers to eliminate the complexities of manual event handling.

By bridging the gap between theory and practice, Chapter 8 will demonstrate how Knative Eventing operationalizes the EDA concepts covered here, making serverless event-driven applications easy to build, manage, and scale.

8

Knative Eventing and CloudEvents

> ... The world is full of obvious things which nobody by looking ever sees.
>
> *(Sherlock Holmes)*

In the previous chapter, we explored how Event-Driven Architecture (EDA) enables scalable, cost-efficient, and reactive serverless applications. We discussed their core principles, patterns, and challenges. We examined how EDAs decouple producers and consumers, enabling scalable, responsive, and resilient systems. Now, we move from theory to practice, focusing on how Knative Eventing brings these architectural principles to life within the Kubernetes ecosystem. Implementing EDA effectively in a Kubernetes-based serverless environment requires the right tools and abstractions. This is where Knative Eventing comes in.

This chapter explores how Knative Eventing turns Kubernetes into a fully serverless event-driven platform, enabling stateless, ephemeral event processing at scale. Additionally, we will learn about CloudEvents, a CNCF specification for standardized event data, enhances interoperability in event-driven systems by enabling services to exchange events in a consistent format. Together, Knative Eventing and CloudEvents simplify the complexities of building scalable, interoperable, and resilient event-driven applications.

This chapter serves as a bridge, connecting the architectural patterns from Chapter 7 to their implementation with Knative. By the end of this chapter, you'll be able to:

- Describe the core components of Knative Eventing and how they work together.
- Configure Knative Eventing components such as Sources, Brokers, Triggers, Channels, and Subscriptions.
- Understand CloudEvents and their role in standardizing event-driven communication.
- Ensure interoperability with CloudEvents, reducing integration overhead.
- Implement advanced features like Dead Letter Queues, Retries, Delivery Guarantees.
- Understand Knative Eventing extensions.

As we progress, you'll see how Knative Eventing operationalizes the foundational principles of EDA, making it easier to build and maintain complex event-driven systems in cloud-native environments. Let's dive into how Knative Eventing brings EDA from concept to reality.

8.1 Exploring Knative Eventing

Traditional event-driven systems require pre-provisioned messaging infrastructure, complex broker management, and static scaling policies — all of which introduce operational overhead. Knative Eventing removes these constraints, bringing serverless scalability to event-driven architectures. Instead of managing dedicated message brokers, event queues, or pre-provisioning compute capacity, Knative dynamically routes and scales event-driven workloads on Kubernetes. By leveraging Knative Eventing, you can:

- Ingest events without persistent infrastructure, eliminating the need to manage message brokers.

- Dynamically scale event consumers to zero when idle, optimizing cost efficiency.

- Standardize event payloads with CloudEvents, ensuring seamless portability across cloud providers and services.

Serverless applications rely on dynamic execution and ephemeral compute, making real-time event-driven communication critical. However, managing event flow manually in Kubernetes — setting up brokers, routing logic, and ensuring delivery — can be highly complex. Knative Eventing abstracts these complexities, providing a Kubernetes-native framework for handling event-driven workflows in a scalable and serverless-friendly way.

Knative Eventing simplifies the delivery of events from producers to consumers, enabling services to react to changes in their environment or state without direct coupling. It simplifies complex event routing, delivering a robust foundation for building an event-driven system. It provides a structured way to handle cloud-native event-driven commu-

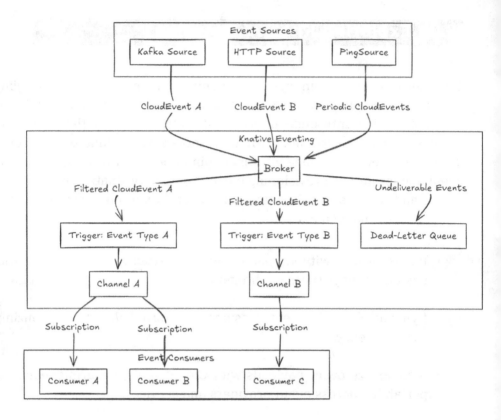

Figure 8.1: Key Components and Event Flow in EDA

nication. Figure 8.1 illustrates this event flow, where event sources produce CloudEvents, which are routed through a Broker, filtered via Triggers, and delivered to consumers via Channels. This model enables seamless event routing in serverless applications. Knative Eventing offers a set of pre-built components that handle event generation, routing, and delivery. It comprises sources for event generation, Brokers for event ingestion, Triggers for event filtering and dispatching, and Channels for secure event transportation. Let's explore these components in detail.

8.2 Event Sources

Event Sources act as the starting point for event generation. Event Sources are responsible for bringing external events into the Knative ecosystem. They represent anything that can produce an event, such as:

- *Microservices*: A service within your application might generate an event when a specific action occurs (e.g., "order placed").

- *External Systems*: Events can also originate from external systems like databases, message queues (e.g., Kafka topics), or webhooks from third-party services.

Common Knative event sources include:

- HTTP Sources: Allow applications to trigger events by sending HTTP POST requests.

- Kafka Sources: Consume events from existing Kafka topics and integrate them into your serverless workflows.

- Cloud Storage Sources: Generate events when files are uploaded or modified in a Cloud Storage bucket.

In a serverless architecture, functions should execute only in response to real-world events, eliminating idle compute. Knative Eventing Sources enable this by integrating external event producers — such as Kafka topics, webhooks, or cloud storage changes — directly into the serverless execution model.

8.3 Configuring Event Sources in Knative

Knative Eventing supports a variety of event sources out of the box. Let's explore some common types of event sources and the configuration steps involved, ensuring a consistent understanding and setup process.

8.3.1 Kafka

You might want to consume events from an existing Apache Kafka topic and integrate them into your Knative-powered event-driven workflows. Kafka is a popular distributed streaming platform often used in EDAs for its scalability and fault-tolerance. To set up Kafka as an event source in Knative, you would define a `KafkaSource` resource. This resource specifies how Knative connects to your Kafka cluster and which topics to consume events from. In our e-commerce workflow, imagine we need to react to order placement events already being published to a Kafka topic. The following `KafkaSource` configuration demonstrates how to listen for messages from the `order-events` topic and forward them to the `order-processing-service` within Knative. It also includes a dead-letter sink for handling undeliverable events, ensuring robustness.

```
apiVersion: sources.knative.dev/v1
kind: KafkaSource
metadata:
  name: order-events-source
  namespace: ecommerce
spec:
  consumerGroup: order-consumer-group
  bootstrapServers:
    - my-kafka-bootstrap.kafka:9092
  topics:
    - order-events
  sink:
    ref:
      apiVersion: serving.knative.dev/v1
```

```
15    kind: Service
16    name: order-processing-service
17  mode: Consumer
18  delivery:
19    retry: 5
20    backoffPolicy: exponential
21    backoffDelay: PT3S
22    deadLetterSink:
23    ref:
24        apiVersion: serving.knative.dev/v1
25        kind: Service
26        name: dlq-service
```

Listing 8.1: KafkaSource YAML Example

This YAML configuration defines a KafkaSource named order-events-source in the ecommerce namespace. Key specifications include: bootstrapServers to point to your Kafka brokers, topics listing the Kafka topics to consume from (order-events in this case), and sink defining the Knative Service (order-processing-service) that will receive the events. The delivery section configures retry attempts and specifies a deadLetterSink (dlq-service) for failed deliveries, ensuring message durability and error handling.

8.3.2 RabbitMQ

Similar to Kafka, you might want to leverage RabbitMQ as a message broker and consume events from RabbitMQ queues within your Knative environment. RabbitMQ is another widely adopted message broker known for its flexible routing and message queuing capabilities. To set up RabbitMQ as an event source, you would define a RabbitmqSource resource. This resource specifies connection details to your RabbitMQ instance and the queues to listen to. Consider a scenario where order updates are published to a RabbitMQ exchange. The following RabbitmqSource example shows how to connect to a RabbitMQ queue and forward messages as CloudEvents to the `rabbitmq-source-sink` Knative Service.

```yaml
1  apiVersion: sources.knative.dev/v1alpha1
2  kind: RabbitmqSource
3  metadata:
4    name: rabbitmq-source
5  spec:
6    connectionSecret:
7      name: test-secret
8    rabbitmqResourcesConfig:
9      exchangeName: "eventing-rabbitmq-source"
10     queueName: "eventing-rabbitmq-source"
11   sink:
12     ref:
13       apiVersion: serving.knative.dev/v1
14       kind: Service
15       name: rabbitmq-source-sink
16       namespace: source-demo
```

Listing 8.2: RabbitmqSource YAML Example

This YAML defines a `RabbitmqSource` named `rabbitmq-source`. Key specifications include: `connectionSecret` which refers to a Kubernetes secret containing RabbitMQ connection credentials, and `rabbitmqResourcesConfig` to specify the `exchangeName` and `queueName` to consume messages from. The `sink` again points to the destination Knative Service, `rabbitmq-source-sink` in this example, where the RabbitMQ messages, converted to CloudEvents, will be delivered for processing. RabbitMQ event sources provide a robust way to integrate Knative with applications already using RabbitMQ as their messaging backbone.

8.3.3 HTTPSource

Imagine you need to trigger event workflows directly via HTTP requests. HTTPSource in Knative Eventing allows you to expose an HTTP endpoint that can accept incoming HTTP POST requests and convert them into CloudEvents. This is particularly useful for integrating with systems that can trigger actions via simple HTTP calls or for creating publicly accessible event entry points. Consider creating an endpoint that can trigger a processing workflow whenever an external partner sends a notification via an HTTP POST request. The following HttpSource configuration sets up an HTTP endpoint that, upon receiving POST requests, will generate CloudEvents and forward them to the event-processor-service.

```yaml
apiVersion: sources.knative.dev/v1beta1
kind: HttpSource
metadata:
  name: http-event-source
  namespace: ecommerce
spec:
  sink:
    ref:
      apiVersion: serving.knative.dev/v1
      kind: Service
      name: event-processor-service
  delivery:
    retry: 3
    backoffPolicy: linear
    backoffDelay: PT2S
    deadLetterSink:
      ref:
        apiVersion: serving.knative.dev/v1
        kind: Service
        name: dlq-service
```

Listing 8.3: HTTPSource YAML Example

This YAML configuration defines an HttpSource named http-event-source. The essential part is the spec.sink, which specifies that events generated by this HTTP source will be sent to the event-processor-service Knative Service. The delivery section includes retry configurations and a deadLetterSink, similar to the Kafka example, providing reliability and error handling for event delivery. With HTTPSource, you can easily create publicly accessible or internal HTTP endpoints that act as event producers in your Knative event-driven system.

Once the HttpSource is deployed, you can trigger it by sending an HTTP POST request to its service endpoint. For the http-event-source in the ecommerce namespace, you can typically send a request within your Kubernetes cluster using a command like this:

```
curl -X POST \
  http://http-event-source.ecommerce.svc.cluster.local \
  -H 'Content-Type: application/json' \
  -d '{"orderID": "1234ABC", "status": "ordered"}'
```

Listing 8.4: Triggering HTTPSource with curl

Knative Eventing offers a versatile framework for event-driven architectures, supporting a wide range of event sources and sinks. While we've explored Kafka and RabbitMQ, Knative also enables you to integrate with various other systems:

- HTTP Sources and Sinks: Easily trigger events based on HTTP requests or send event payloads via HTTP.

- Cloud Storage Sources: Monitor changes in cloud storage buckets (e.g., Google Cloud Storage, Azure Blob Storage) and generate events accordingly.

- Message Queues: Integrate with message queues like RabbitMQ or Amazon SQS to seamlessly exchange events.

- **Custom Sources and Sinks:** Leverage Knative's extensibility to create custom sources and sinks tailored to your specific needs.

The exact configuration format and available options might vary slightly depending on the specific source type. By providing this flexibility, Knative empowers you to build complex, event-driven systems that can adapt to various use cases and integration scenarios.

Now that we've seen how external events (from Kafka topics or HTTP sources) can enter our cluster via Knative Event Sources, the next step is deciding where those events should go and how they should be delivered. Knative offers two primary routing mechanismsBrokers/Triggers and Channels/Subscriptionseach suited to different scenarios. Let's explore both approaches in detail

8.4 Event Routing Mechanisms

Knative Eventing offers two distinct approaches to routing events: **Brokers and Triggers** for simpler, centralized routing and **Channels and Subscriptions** for more explicit and feature-rich pipelines. Let's examine each in detail to understand their respective strengths and best use cases.

Brokers and Triggers: Simpler, Centralized Routing

Brokers and Triggers provide a streamlined and centralized approach to event routing within Knative Eventing. They are ideally suited for scenarios where you need a central event hub with flexible, attribute-based routing. Consider using Brokers and Triggers when:

- **Dynamic Routing is Required**: You need routing decisions to be made dynamically based on the attributes of each event. Triggers excel at filtering events based on attributes like type and source, allowing for flexible routing logic without needing to predefine rigid pathways.

- **Fan-Out with Filtering is Essential**: You want to distribute the same event to multiple consumer services, but each service is interested in only a specific subset of events. Triggers allow you to define filters so that each service receives only the events it needs, efficiently utilizing resources and simplifying service logic.

- **Simplified Initial Setup is Preferred**: For basic event routing needs, Brokers and Triggers offer a simpler initial configuration compared to Channels and Subscriptions. They abstract away some of the underlying complexities, making them a good starting point for many event-driven applications.

The key advantages of Brokers and Triggers lie in their abstraction of routing logic and dynamic filtering capabilities. Brokers act as central event hubs, while Triggers define flexible rules for dispatching events based on their characteristics. Although Brokers internally utilize Channels for event delivery, this detail is largely hidden, providing a more user-friendly experience for common routing tasks.

Channels and Subscriptions: Explicit, Feature-Rich Pipelines

In contrast to Brokers and Triggers, Channels and Subscriptions offer a more explicit and feature-rich approach to event routing. They are the preferred choice when you require greater control over event delivery, need durable event storage, or want to leverage advanced messaging features. Opt for Channels and Subscriptions when:

- **Durable Event Storage is Necessary**: You require persistent event storage for reliability and potential event replay. Channels like KafkaChannel provide backing by robust messaging systems like Kafka, ensuring events are durably stored and can be replayed if needed.

- **Fine-grained Control Over Delivery Guarantees is Critical**: You need to explicitly configure delivery guarantees, such as at-least-once or at-most-once, and fine-tune retry policies. Channels and Subscriptions offer detailed settings to manage these aspects, allowing precise control over reliability and message processing behavior.

- **Complex Event Flows are Involved**: Your application requires chaining channels, transforming events as they flow through pipelines, or creating intricate routing topologies that go beyond simple filtering. Channels and Subscriptions provide the building blocks for constructing these more sophisticated event flows.

- **Fan-Out without Broker-Level Filtering is Needed**: You need to broadcast events to multiple consumers without relying on the Broker's filtering capabilities. Alternatively, you may prefer to handle more complex filtering logic within the application services themselves, in which case Channels and Subscriptions provide a more direct event delivery mechanism to each service.

Channels and Subscriptions offer key advantages in their explicit control over event pipelines, durable storage options, and configurable delivery guarantees. They are more verbose in configuration and slightly more complex to set up initially compared to Brokers and Triggers, but this explicitness provides significant power and flexibility for advanced event-driven scenarios.

Choosing the Right Event Routing Mechanism

Choosing between Brokers/Triggers and Channels/Subscriptions depends largely on the specific needs of your project. For many applications, especially in the early stages, Brokers and Triggers provide an excellent starting point due to their simplicity and centralized routing capabilities. They are well-suited for scenarios where dynamic, attribute-based filtering and basic fan-out are the primary requirements. However, as your event-driven architecture evolves and your needs become more complexperhaps requiring durable event storage, stricter delivery guarantees, or intricate event flow patterns — Channels and Subscriptions offer the necessary flexibility and control. They are ideal for mission-critical workflows where reliability, data persistence, and advanced messaging features are paramount.

In practice, many projects may begin with Brokers/Triggers for their initial simplicity and then transition to Channels/Subscriptions in parts of their system as requirements for reliability and control increase. Both routing mechanisms are valuable tools within Knative Eventing, and the "best" choice is determined by the specific demands of your application, workflow, and desired level of control over event delivery.

Let's now begin our detailed exploration of these routing mechanisms, starting with Brokers and Triggers and their role in simplifying event distribution.

8.5 Brokers and Triggers

Brokers serve as an event hub, receiving events from various sources and making them available to consumers. They provide an abstraction layer between event producers and consumers, promoting loose coupling. Depending on configuration, Brokers can offer different delivery guaranteessuch as at least once (ensuring events are delivered) or exactly once (eliminating duplicates). Knative automates the complexity of managing Brokers, making event routing seamless.

Triggers define the conditions for routing events from Brokers to specific consumers. Each Trigger filters events based on attributes like event type and source, ensuring that only relevant events are sent to the appropriate services. Multiple Triggers can subscribe to the same Broker, allowing the same event to be processed by different services independently.

Knative's Broker-Trigger mechanism simplifies event routing by dynamically directing events to serverless workloads, ensuring functions execute only when needed.

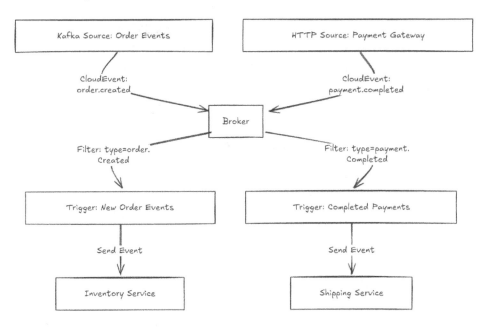

Figure 8.2: Workflow with Brokers and Triggers

Figure 8.2 depicts a real-world event-driven workflow in an e-commerce system. The Kafka source emits `order.created` events, which are routed to an Inventory Service, while HTTP-based payment.completed events trigger the Shipping Service. The Kafka source emits `order.created` events and the HTTP source emits `payment.completed` events. These events are sent to a Broker, which acts as the event distribution hub. Triggers are then used to filter events based on their type (e.g., order.created and payment.completed), ensuring they are routed to the appropriate services, such as Inventory Service and Shipping Service. This workflow enables scalable and loosely coupled event-driven processing within Kubernetes. This event-driven approach ensures that the Inventory and Shipping services only execute when triggered by their respective events, optimizing resource usage and aligning with the serverless pay-per-use model.

The listing 8.5 below provides the YAML definition for the `New Order Events Trigger` depicted in Figure 8.2 . This Trigger filters for events of type `order.created` and routes them to the `inventory-service`, demonstrating how Triggers enable precise event routing in Knative Eventing.

```yaml
---
# Define the Broker
apiVersion: eventing.knative.dev/v1
kind: Broker
metadata:
  name: order-events-broker
  namespace: ecommerce
spec: {}
---
# Define the Trigger for Order Created Events
apiVersion: eventing.knative.dev/v1
kind: Trigger
metadata:
  name: new-order-trigger
  namespace: ecommerce
spec:
  broker: order-events-broker
```

```
18  filter:
19    attributes:
20      type: order.created
21  subscriber:
22    ref:
23      apiVersion: serving.knative.dev/v1
24      kind: Service
25      name: inventory-service
26  delivery:
27    retry: 3
28    backoffPolicy: exponential
29    backoffDelay: PT5S
30    deadLetterSink:
31      ref:
32        apiVersion: serving.knative.dev/v1
33        kind: Service
34        name: dlq-service
```

Listing 8.5: YAML Example

Key responsibilities of brokers and triggers are

- Event Ingestion: Brokers receive events from diverse sources and acknowledge their successful reception.

- Event Filtering: Triggers can be configured to optionally filter events based on specific criteria before forwarding them. This reduces unnecessary processing for consumer services.

- Routing: Brokers play a crucial role in routing events to the appropriate consumers. They rely on triggers to determine which events each consumer is interested in.

Brokers and Triggers provide a powerful mechanism for routing events to their intended destinations. While this approach works well for many scenarios, there are cases where you need more control over event delivery, persistence, and routing. This is where Channels and

Subscriptions step in to provide explicit routing, persistence, and fan-out delivery.

8.6 Channels and Subscriptions

Channels serve as reliable delivery pipelines within Knative Eventing. Channels act as directed pathways or pipelines for transporting events from Brokers to Subscribers. They offer features like durable storage, fan-out to multiple consumers, and delivery guarantees to ensure that events reach their intended destinations reliably. While some Channels offer `at-least-once delivery`, achieving `exactly-once` delivery semantics often requires more complex mechanisms, such as idempotent message processing or distributed transaction management, which are not directly provided by Knative Eventing. The choice depends on your application's specific requirements for data consistency. Knative offers different built-in channel types. The channel type influences delivery guarantees. The `InMemoryChannel` is a simple built-in channel for basic scenarios when you do not need events to be persisted. Another one is `KafkaChannel`, which is backed by Kafka topics, offering persistence, scalability, and replay capabilities. You can chain Channels, with output from one Channel becoming input to another, enabling intricate event flows. Services receiving events from a Channel might transform them (adding or removing attributes) before forwarding them along to another Channel.

The choice between using Brokers/Triggers and Channels/Subscriptions depends on the specific needs of your event-driven architecture. If you require durable event storage, fan-out capabilities, or delivery guarantees, then Channels/Subscriptions are the way to go. However, if you have simpler routing needs and don't require these advanced features, then Brokers/Triggers offer a more lightweight and efficient solution.

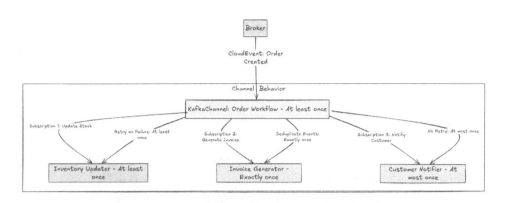

Figure 8.3: Channels and Subscriptions in Knative Eventing

Figure 8.3 illustrates the interaction between Channels and Subscriptions in the order processing pipeline of our eCommerce system. Figure 8.3 highlights how events are routed and delivered to various consumers and highlights how delivery guarantees are applied based on task criticality. Events flow through a KafkaChannel, which acts as the central pipeline managing the reliable routing and processing of events related to new orders. Each consumer has a specific responsibility, and its delivery guarantee is tailored to the importance of its task.

The Inventory Updater service processes events from the KafkaChannel to adjust stock levels for items in the order. For this service, an at-least-once delivery guarantee is configured. This ensures that every event is processed at least once, preventing stock discrepancies caused by missed events. However, duplicates may occur if the system retries a failed event. To handle this, the Inventory Updater uses idempotent processing, ensuring stock adjustments for an order are only applied once based on the unique order ID.

Next, the Invoice Generator is responsible for generating and sending invoices to customers. Since duplicate invoices can lead to billing errors and confusion, achieving exactly-once processing is crucial. However, Knative Eventing does not enforce exactly-once delivery natively; it only guarantees at-least-once delivery. To ensure that each invoice is processed exactly once, the Invoice Generator implements deduplication logic at the application level. It can do this by implementing idempotent operations or tracking processed events to prevent duplicates. This approach ensures that customers receive accurate invoices without the risk of overcharging.

Finally, the Customer Notifier sends email or SMS notifications to customers confirming their orders. Since these notifications are non-critical, an at-most-once delivery guarantee is applied. This means the event is delivered once, if possible, but no retries are performed if delivery fails. This approach minimizes resource usage for non-essential operations, prioritizing critical workflows instead.

The KafkaChannel's delivery behavior reflects these guarantees. Events routed to the Inventory Updater are retried on failure to ensure reliability, aligning with its at-least-once delivery guarantee. For the Invoice Generator, the channel ensures deduplication, supporting the exactly-once guarantee. For the Customer Notifier, no retries are performed, adhering to its at-most-once delivery guarantee. This setup balances system reliability, efficiency, and complexity based on the criticality of each task.

8.6.1 Configuring Channels & Subscriptions

To illustrate the above flow, lets start by defining a KafkaChannel that will handle our e-commerce order events:

```
apiVersion: messaging.knative.dev/v1
kind: KafkaChannel
metadata:
  name: order-events-channel
spec:
  numPartitions: 3  # Number of partitions for scalability
```

```
7   replicationFactor: 2   # Replication for fault-tolerance
```

Listing 8.6: Kafka Channel Definition Example

This configuration creates a KafkaChannel named `order-events-channel` with three partitions for scalability and a replication factor of two for fault tolerance.

Subscriptions define the linkage between a Channel and a specific Knative Service or other addressable targets. A single Channel can have multiple Subscriptions, enabling fan-out scenarios where events are delivered to multiple consumers. Subscriptions can include options such as retry settings, which manage how failed event deliveries are retried, and Dead Letter Sink, which specifies where events are sent if delivery ultimately fails.

To illustrate how Knative Eventing enables reliable event delivery, we define Subscriptions that connect our order-events-channel to various services responsible for handling order events. These configurations ensure durability, retries, and error handling.

```
1  # Inventory Updater Subscription (At-Least-Once)
2  apiVersion: messaging.knative.dev/v1
3  kind: Subscription
4  metadata:
5    name: inventory-updater-subscription
6  spec:
7    channel:
8      ref:
9        name: order-events-channel
10   subscriber:
11     ref:
12       apiVersion: serving.knative.dev/v1
13       kind: Service
14       name: inventory-service
15   delivery:
16     retry: 5
17     backoffPolicy: exponential
```

```
18    backoffDelay: PT5S
19    deadLetterSink:
20      ref:
21        apiVersion: serving.knative.dev/v1
22        kind: Service
23        name: dead-letter-queue-service  # Stores events that
      failed even after retries
```

Listing 8.7: Inventory Service Subscription

This Subscription ensures that events from the order-events-channel are delivered to the inventory-service. It also includes a deadLetterSink to handle any failed deliveries, ensuring no events are lost.

Similarly, we can define another Subscription to connect the same order-events-channel to the invoice-service, demonstrating the fan-out capability where multiple consumers can receive events from the same channel.

The Invoice Generator service must ensure that an invoice is generated exactly once per order, avoiding duplicate billing issues. To enforce this, the service implements deduplication logic, rather than relying on Knative to enforce exactly-once semantics. If an event delivery ultimately fails, it is sent to the dead-letter queue (DLQ) for further analysis.

```
1  # Invoice Generator Subscription (At-Least-Once with Deduplication)
2  apiVersion: messaging.knative.dev/v1
3  kind: Subscription
4  metadata:
5    name: invoice-generator-subscription
6    namespace: ecommerce
7  spec:
8    channel:
9      ref:
10        name: order-events-channel
11    subscriber:
12      ref:
```

```
13      apiVersion: serving.knative.dev/v1
14      kind: Service
15      name: invoice-service
16    delivery:
17      deadLetterSink:
18        ref:
19          apiVersion: serving.knative.dev/v1
20          kind: Service
21          name: dlq-service  # Captures failed invoices for manual
      resolution
```

Listing 8.8: Invoice Generator Subscriber

The Customer Notifier service sends email or SMS notifications to customers when their order is placed. Since these notifications are non-critical (i.e., if a notification fails, it does not impact the business logic of the order), an at-most-once delivery guarantee is applied. This means that the event is delivered once, if possible, but no retries are performed if delivery fails. This approach minimizes resource usage for non-essential operations, prioritizing critical workflows instead.

```
1  # Customer Notifier Subscription (At-Most-Once)
2  apiVersion: messaging.knative.dev/v1
3  kind: Subscription
4  metadata:
5    name: customer-notifier-subscription
6    namespace: ecommerce
7  spec:
8    channel:
9      ref:
10        name: order-events-channel
11    subscriber:
12      ref:
13        apiVersion: serving.knative.dev/v1
14        kind: Service
15        name: customer-notifier-service
```

Listing 8.9: Customer Notifier Subscriber

By implementing Channels and Subscriptions in this way, we ensure that event-driven workflows remain resilient, scalable, and maintainable.

8.7 Advanced Knative Eventing Features

This section delves into advanced Knative Eventing features that can significantly enhance the resilience, scalability, and adaptability of your event-driven applications. These features include Dead Letter Queues (DLQs), Delivery Guarantees, and Knative Eventing extensions.

8.7.1 Dead Letter Queues (DLQs)

Inherent to message-driven systems is the possibility of message delivery failures. These failures can stem from transient network hiccups, subscriber unavailability, or even glitches within the subscriber's logic. Knative addresses this challenge with Dead Letter Queues (DLQs), a mechanism designed to capture and manage these undelivered messages. When an event fails to reach its intended subscriber, Knative can be configured to redirect it to a DLQ. This DLQ can be any addressable endpoint that adheres to the Knative Eventing sink contract, encompassing Knative Services, Kubernetes Services, or external URIs. This flexibility allows for diverse integration options and centralized management of failed events.

Configuring a DLQ involves specifying the deadLetterSink within the delivery spec of your Broker or Subscription. This spec also provides granular control over retry behavior, allowing you to define the number of retry attempts before an event is relegated to the DLQ using the retry configuration. Additionally, you can fine-tune the retry mechanism by setting the backoffDelay and backoffPolicy parameters.

Consider this example of a Broker configuration with a DLQ:

```
apiVersion: eventing.knative.dev/v1
kind: Broker
metadata:
  name: with-dead-letter-sink
spec:
  delivery:
    deadLetterSink:
      ref:
        apiVersion: serving.knative.dev/v1
        kind: Service
        name: example-sink
```

Listing 8.10: YAML Example

In this scenario, any event failing delivery through this Broker will be routed to the example-sink Service. Furthermore, each dead letter event carries valuable debugging information in the form of knativeerrorcode and knativeerrordata attributes. The knativeerrorcode provides the HTTP response status code from the final delivery attempt, while knativeerrordata contains the HTTP response body, offering insights into the nature of the failure. In this scenario, any event failing delivery through this Broker will be routed to the example-sink Service. Furthermore, each dead letter event carries valuable debugging information in the form of knativeerrorcode and knativeerrordata attributes. The knativeerrorcode provides the HTTP response status code from the final delivery attempt, while knativeerrordata contains the HTTP response body, offering insights into the nature of the failure.

DLQs offer several key advantages:

- Prevent Message Loss: DLQs act as a safety net, ensuring that even failed messages are preserved, allowing for subsequent investigation and potential reprocessing.

- Improve System Reliability: By gracefully handling delivery failures, DLQs prevent errors from propagating through the system, bolstering overall reliability.

- Enable Debugging and Monitoring: DLQs provide a centralized repository for inspecting failed events, simplifying debugging efforts and facilitating system health monitoring.

8.7.2 Delivery Guarantees

Knative offers varying levels of delivery guarantees depending on the chosen Channel type. These guarantees dictate how messages are delivered to subscribers and the system's behavior in the face of failures. Knative supports three primary delivery guarantees:

- At-most-once: This guarantee ensures a message is delivered to the subscriber no more than once. However, it does not guarantee delivery, and messages may be lost in case of failures.

- At-least-once: This guarantee ensures a message is delivered to the subscriber at least once. While preventing message loss, it may lead to duplicate deliveries if a failure occurs after the subscriber processes the message but before the system acknowledges successful delivery.

- Exactly-once: This is the most stringent guarantee, ensuring each message is delivered to the subscriber precisely once, without any loss or duplication. Achieving this typically involves more complex mechanisms like idempotent message processing or distributed transaction management.

Different Channel implementations in Knative offer distinct delivery guarantees. For instance, the default InMemoryChannel provides at-most-once delivery, where the event is delivered no more than once but might be lost in case of failures. In contrast, the KafkaChannel supports ordered consumer delivery, offering an at-least-once guarantee within a partition. It's crucial to select a Channel type that aligns with your application's delivery guarantee requirements.

Knative offers two delivery methods: simple and complex. Simple delivery involves a direct connection between the event source and the service, offering no delivery guarantees. Complex delivery, on the other hand, leverages Channels and Subscriptions, enabling at-least-once delivery guarantees and 1:n fanout capabilities. The RetryAfterMax field in the delivery spec plays a crucial role in enforcing retry-after headers. This field interacts with feature flags to control how the system handles retry attempts based on the subscriber's response. When enabled, it enforces retry-after headers, allowing subscribers to influence the retry behavior.

The choice of delivery guarantee hinges on your application's specific needs. For applications where occasional message loss is tolerable, at-most-once delivery might suffice. However, mission-critical applications demanding high reliability and data integrity necessitate at-least-once or exactly-once delivery. It's important to recognize the trade-off between delivery guarantees and performance. Stronger guarantees often entail increased overhead and potentially reduced performance. Carefully consider this trade-off when selecting the appropriate guarantee for your application.

The delivery spec allows fine-grained control over delivery guarantees. It includes options for specifying dead-letter sinks, retry policies (number of retries, backoff delay, backoff policy), and delivery order guarantees. For instance, with the Kafka Broker, you can use annotations like `kafka.eventing.knative.dev/delivery.order` to control message ordering

8.7.3   Knative Eventing Extensions

Knative Eventing provides a framework for extending its core functionality. These extensions enable integration with diverse third-party
systems, the addition of custom features, and the tailoring of Knative to
specific requirements. Knative extensions can be categorized into:

- Sources: Extensions that facilitate event ingestion from various
  sources, such as databases, message queues, or cloud services.

- Channels: Extensions that offer alternative Channel implementations with different delivery guarantees or performance characteristics.

- Brokers: Extensions that provide different Broker implementations, potentially with specialized features or integrations.

- Queue Extensions: Extensions that modify the behavior of the
  queue proxy, potentially influencing queuing, dispatch, and retry
  mechanisms.

- Plugins: Extensions to the kn CLI tool that provide additional
  commands and functionalities.

The Knative community actively develops and maintains a variety of
extensions, including:

- Knative Kafka Broker: An alternative Broker implementation that
  utilizes Apache Kafka as the underlying messaging system.

- RabbitMQ Eventing components: Source and Broker extensions for
  integrating with RabbitMQ.

- Knative Quickstart Plugin: A plugin for the kn CLI that streamlines the installation of a Knative cluster for development purposes.

Extensions offer several key benefits:

- Increased Flexibility: Extensions empower you to adapt Knative to a broader spectrum of use cases and integrate it seamlessly with your existing infrastructure.

- Enhanced Functionality: Extensions can introduce features not present in the core Knative Eventing platform, enriching its capabilities.

- Community-Driven Innovation: The vibrant Knative community actively develops and maintains a diverse array of extensions, fostering innovation and collaboration.

Extensions are a crucial mechanism for customizing and adapting Knative to specific requirements. They allow you to tailor Knative to diverse use cases and integrate it with existing systems, enhancing its versatility and adaptability.

8.8 Understanding CloudEvents

In large-scale distributed systems, services often communicate by sending and receiving events. However, a lack of standardization in how these events are structured can lead to complexity for developers. Services need to have specific knowledge of the different event formats used by other parts of the system, increasing developer overhead and potential for errors. Monitoring, debugging, and building event routing infrastructure becomes complicated when dealing with a multitude of event formats.

With the proliferation of event-driven architectures, the need for a common way to describe event data has become apparent. CloudEvents, a project under the Cloud Native Computing Foundation (CNCF), aims to standardize the specification of event data, promoting interoperability across services, platforms, and systems. The specification designed to describe event data in a common and consistent way. Think of it as a standardized envelope format for events, ensuring different systems can easily understand and exchange them. This specification brings several key advantages:

- Standardizes event metadata (e.g., event type, source, timestamp), making it easier for services to consume events without custom parsing logic.

- Works across cloud providers and messaging systems (e.g., Kafka, HTTP, AMQP), preventing vendor lock-in.

- Enables seamless event routing in Knative, ensuring that events can be dynamically processed using Brokers, Triggers, and Channels.

- Simplified Tooling: Common libraries, brokers, and event visualization tools can be built to work with any CloudEvent, reducing effort and complexity in event-driven architectures.

8.8.1 Structure of a CloudEvent

CloudEvents provides a vendor-neutral specification that defines a set of core metadata attributes for describing events. A CloudEvent is designed to carry all the necessary information about an event, making it easily understandable and usable across different systems. Key attributes include:

- `specversion` (string): The version of the CloudEvents specification being used (e.g., 1.0).

- `type` (string): The type of the event related to the originating occurrence (e.g., order.placed, product.inventory_updated, customer.created). This is central to understanding the event's nature.

- `source` (URIreference): A URI identifying the context where the event happened. This could be a specific service, application, or device.

- `id` (string): A unique identifier that distinguishes this specific event instance from others.

- `time` (string, optional): A timestamp when the event occurred.

- `datacontenttype` (string, optional): The content type of the event data. (e.g., application/json, text/xml)

- `data` : The actual event data payload, which can be of any format and is where the event's specific information is contained.

Additionally, CloudEvents supports extensions for adding additional metadata that might be required for certain processing scenarios, providing flexibility while maintaining interoperability. These extensions can be

Custom Extensions: You can create your own extensions to add specific information relevant to your application domain in an event. An example of a custom extension is an order_total attribute for an order event.

Standard Extensions: The CloudEvents community is working on standard extensions for common scenarios, like tracing or distributed correlation IDs.

A json based example of an order placed cloud event is below. This CloudEvent, on its own, provides essential information about the occurrence of an order. In a real-world system, it would likely trigger other events (inventory updates, payment processing, etc.).

```
1  {
2      "specversion": "1.0",
3      "type": "com.example.ecommerce.order.placed",
4      "source": "/ecommerce/orders",
5      "id": "A234-123456-BCDEF",
6      "time": "2023-12-10T18:25:15-05:00",
7      "datacontenttype": "application/json",
8      "data": {
9          "order_id": "123456",
10         "customer_id": "user-1001",
11         "items": [
12             { "product_id": "XYZ-123", "quantity": 2 },
13             { "product_id": "ABC-789", "quantity": 1 }
14         ],
15         "total_amount": 99.99
16     }
17 }
```

Listing 8.11: JSON Example

8.8.2 Bindings

Bindings are the mechanisms that define how CloudEvents are represented when sent over different protocols or messaging systems such as HTTP, Kafka, AMQP, and others. It defines how to map its properties to these standard protocols. This ensures that CloudEvents can be easily sent and received across different messaging systems without losing their meaning or requiring custom parsing logic. Your application components don't need to care about the underlying transport mechanism — they simply produce and consume standard CloudEvents. Services using any of these different communication protocols can still seamlessly exchange events.

Bindings define rules for how to serialize the CloudEvent's attributes and data into a format suitable for the specific protocol (e.g., HTTP headers and body, Kafka message payload). It also specifies how to deserialize and extract the CloudEvent's structure back from the protocol-specific representation. Bindings can be Structured or Binary. Structured bindings (e.g., with HTTP) represent the CloudEvent attributes in readable formats like JSON or XML. Binary bindings (e.g., with Kafka) aim to optimize for smaller message sizes and better performance. The CloudEvents project maintains specifications for standard bindings with common protocols. You can potentially define your own bindings for specialized protocols if needed. An example of a structured binding within an HTTP POST is below

```
 1 POST /my-webhook-endpoint HTTP/1.1
 2 Content-Type: application/cloudevents+json
 3 {
 4     specversion: 1.0,
 5     type: com.example.ecommerce.order.placed,
 6     id: A234-123456-BCDEF,
 7     time: 2023-12-10T18:25:15-05:00,
 8     datacontenttype: application/json,
 9     data: {
10         order_id: 123456,
11         customer_id: user-1001,
12         items: [
13             { product_id: XYZ-123, quantity: 2 },
14             { product_id: ABC-789, quantity: 1 }
15         ],
16         total_amount: 99.99
17     }
18 }
```

Listing 8.12: CloudEvents — HTTP POST Binding

8.8.3 SDKs

To facilitate working with CloudEvents across various programming environments, the Cloud Native Computing Foundation provides SDKs for languages including C#, Go, JavaScript, Python, and others. These SDK's provide libraries and tools that abstract away the complexities of working directly with CloudEvent specifications and bindings. They handle attribute encoding and serialization according to the standard. Conversely, they also help parse incoming CloudEvents received from different sources. Many SDKs include support for common bindings such as HTTP, Kafka, and others. They automate the serialization and deserialization of CloudEvents for these protocols, so you don't have to worry about encoding details. SDKs save you from manually crafting CloudEvents and let you focus on the core logic of your services, streamlining the event-driven development process. For .NET developers, including the `CloudNative.CloudEvents` nuget package simplifies creating, parsing, and publishing CloudEvents, making it seamless to integrate with Knative Eventing or any other CloudEvents-compliant system. A simple example of creating an Order placed CloudEvent in.NET is below.

```
1  using CloudNative.CloudEvents; // Assuming you've included a.NET
       SDK
2
3  var cloudEvent = new CloudEvent
4  {
5      Type = com.example.ecommerce.order.placed,
6      Source = new Uri(/ecommerce/orders),
7      Id = Guid.NewGuid().ToString(),
8      Time = DateTimeOffset.UtcNow,
9      Data = new { order_id = 12345, customer_id = user-1001,... }
10 };
```

Listing 8.13: Using CloudEvents SDK

8.9 Summary

Knative Eventing and CloudEvents are foundational building blocks for designing modern, event-driven, and cloud-native architectures. By combining the flexibility of Knative Eventing's Kubernetes-native framework with the interoperability of CloudEvents, developers can create scalable, loosely coupled, and robust systems that are resilient to change.

Through this chapter, you have learned:

- How **Knative Eventing** simplifies event routing, delivery, and lifecycle management.

- The role of **Sources, Brokers, Triggers, Channels, and Subscriptions** in creating a complete event-driven ecosystem.

- How **CloudEvents** standardize event data, ensuring interoperability and reducing development overhead.

- Practical configurations and examples to get started with Knative and leverage event-driven design in real-world applications.

- Advanced capabilities like **Dead Letter Queues**, **delivery guarantees**, and **Knative extensions** to enhance system reliability and adaptability.

As the event-driven paradigm continues to grow, leveraging Knative Eventing and CloudEvents provides a future-proof approach to building applications that respond to the dynamic needs of today's cloud-native environments.

8.10 Next Steps

To further solidify your understanding:

1. **Hands-on Practice**: Experiment with deploying a small-scale Knative Eventing setup in your Kubernetes cluster. Start with simple Sources and gradually incorporate Brokers, Triggers, and Channels.

2. **Advanced Workflows**: Explore multi-service workflows by chaining Channels and Triggers to build more complex event pipelines.

3. **Integration**: Investigate how Knative Eventing can integrate with other tools and platforms in your ecosystem, such as Kafka, RabbitMQ, or external webhooks.

4. **Observability**: Learn to monitor and debug your event-driven workflows using Knative's built-in metrics, logging tools, and CloudEvent attributes.

With a solid grounding in Knative Eventing and CloudEvents, we're ready to tackle more sophisticated orchestrations that go beyond simple publish event / consume event flows. In **Chapter 9**, we'll learn how to orchestrate multi-step workflows using advanced features like Knative *Sequences* and *Parallels*, handle errors gracefully with dead letter queues and retry policies, and ensure our event-driven systems remain reliable and transparent at scale.

9

Advanced Orchestration with Knative Eventing

> ... The whole is greater than the sum of its parts.
>
> *(Aristotle)*

In the previous chapters, we explored two crucial building blocks for cloud-native, event-driven applications. Chapter 7 introduced the core principles and patterns of **Event-Driven Architecture (EDA)**, emphasizing the decoupling, scalability, and resilience afforded by asynchronous communication. Chapter 8 then showed how these principles come to life in **Knative Eventing**, leveraging key components such as *Brokers, Triggers, Channels, Sources*, and the *CloudEvents* specification to simplify event routing and standardize event data formats.

This chapter takes the next step by diving into **advanced orchestration techniques** and **real-world applications** of Knative Eventing. Modern cloud-native systems often require dynamic, multi-step workflows where events flow seamlessly across diverse services, with robust handling for failure scenarios, observability, schema evolution, and even multi-tenancy. By learning how to orchestrate these complex workflows with Knative Eventing, you will be able to design, implement, and troubleshoot the kinds of large-scale, mission-critical systems that truly showcase the power of EDA in the cloud.

By the end of this chapter, you will be able to:

- ▸ Orchestrate multi-step workflows using Knative Eventing components.
- ▸ Implement failure-handling strategies such as Dead Letter Queues (DLQs) and retries.
- ▸ Design workflows that support schema evolution and event versioning.
- ▸ Monitor and debug event-driven systems with modern observability tools.
- ▸ Build systems that operate effectively in hybrid and multi-tenant environments.

9.1 Advanced Workflow Orchestration

Recall from Chapter 7 that event-driven systems thrive when services are loosely coupled and communicate asynchronously. In Chapter 8, we introduced Knative Eventing as a Kubernetes-native framework that simplifies event routing. With those concepts in mind, we now move on to orchestrating multiple services into more complex workflows. While basic event routing is valuable, realizing the full potential of EDA often requires orchestrating complex workflows. This is where **Knative Eventing's** strength as an orchestration platform becomes evident. It provides the tools to not just route events, but to actively manage and coordinate multi-step processes in a cloud-native, serverless manner.

Building workflows in event-driven systems involves orchestrating multiple services that work together to achieve a larger goal. Knative Eventing provides a flexible framework for routing events dynamically using Brokers, Triggers, and Channels, as explored in Chapter 8. This section shows how those components can be combinedoften along with Sequences or Parallel flowsto create robust, multi-step workflows.

This approach builds upon the concepts introduced in Chapter 3, where we discussed function design patterns and the implementation of the event-driven pattern. In that section, we illustrated a simplified example of what happens in an e-commerce system when a user clicks the place order button. Each independent function reacts to events and triggers further events based on the program flow, creating a loosely coupled and scalable architecture.

Here, we extend that foundational idea and demonstrate how Knative Eventing's core components - Brokers, Triggers, and Channels - enhance the design and execution of such event-driven workflows by adding robust routing, reliability, and observability.

9.1.1 Function Chaining with Knative Eventing

In Chapter 3, we introduced the **Function Chaining Pattern**, a design pattern for building modular workflows in serverless architectures. Figure 3.2 illustrates this pattern in the context of an e-commerce platform, where a personalized discount generation workflow is triggered when a customer proceeds to checkout.

Knative Eventing provides the tools to streamline this pattern, making it scalable, resilient, and easier to implement. By utilizing Knative Sequences, we can orchestrate the flow of events between functions seamlessly, ensuring reliability and simplifying error handling.

Mapping Functions to Knative Components

Each function in the workflow corresponds to a step in a Knative Sequence:

- **CheckoutFunction**: This function initiates the discount generation process. It retrieves the customer's ID and cart details and then triggers the next function in the sequence.. It starts the process by emitting the initial event (EVENT_ORDER_PLACED) to start the sequence.

- **AnalyzeShoppingHistoryFunction**: This function analyzes the customer's shopping history to determine their eligibility for discounts based on factors like total spending and purchase frequency. It processes the customer's shopping history and emits an analysis event.

- **ReviewCartFunction**: This function reviews the customer's current cart in the context of their shopping history analysis to determine the best possible discount. It considers factors like loyalty tier, eligible products, and ongoing promotions. It combines the cart details and history analysis to determine applicable discounts.

- **GenerateDiscountCodeFunction**: This function generates a personalized discount code for the customer based on the analysis of their shopping history and current cart.

- **ApplyDiscountToCheckoutFunction**: This function applies the generated discount code to the customer's checkout, updating the total cost and optionally confirming the discount application to the customer.

Knative Sequence Configuration

Below is an example of configuring a Knative Sequence to implement this workflow:

```
1  apiVersion: flows.knative.dev/v1
2  kind: Sequence
3  metadata:
4    name: discount-generation-sequence
5  spec:
6    steps:
7      - ref:
8          apiVersion: serving.knative.dev/v1
9          kind: Service
10         name: checkout-service
11     - ref:
12         apiVersion: serving.knative.dev/v1
13         kind: Service
14         name: analyze-shopping-history-service
15     - ref:
16         apiVersion: serving.knative.dev/v1
17         kind: Service
18         name: review-cart-service
19     - ref:
```

```
20        apiVersion: serving.knative.dev/v1
21        kind: Service
22        name: generate-discount-code-service
23      - ref:
24        apiVersion: serving.knative.dev/v1
25        kind: Service
26        name: apply-discount-service
27    channelTemplate:
28      apiVersion: messaging.knative.dev/v1
29      kind: InMemoryChannel
```

Listing 9.1: Knative Sequence for Discount Generation

How Knative Eventing Enables Function Chaining

Knative Eventing enables function chaining primarily through the **Sequence** custom resource that lets you define each step in a linear workflow. In essence, a Sequence routes events through a list of steps (each step typically references a Knative Service) so that the output of one step automatically becomes the input event for the next. The **channelTemplate** section specifies the type of messaging channel to be used for communication within the Sequence. As discussed in (Chapter 8), this provides an abstraction, allowing you to choose the underlying messaging technology (like InMemoryChannel for simplicity or KafkaChannel for production workloads) without changing the core Sequence definition. This flexibility is key to adapting your workflows to different environments and performance needs. Below is a closer look at how it all works:

1. **Sequence CRD (Custom Resource Definition)** Knative provides a *Sequence* object for chaining multiple services. You list out each function in the exact order you want them to run. Under the hood, Knative treats each step as an addressable endpoint—commonly a Knative Service.

2. **Event Passing and Chaining** When the first function finishes processing an event, Knative routes that function's output (a CloudEvent) to the next function in the sequence. This pattern repeats for each step. The beauty here is that you don't have to manually manage any event passing or data transformation in-between; Knative Eventing handles it on your behalf.

3. **Built-In Reliability and Routing** Sequences are powered by `Channels` and `Subscriptions`. These components take care of reliably delivering each event from one step to the next, ensuring *at-least-once* semantics. This built-in reliability is a key benefit of Knative Eventing, freeing developers from having to implement and manage complex message delivery logic themselves. Because the system is event-driven, if one step starts receiving a high volume of events, Knative can autoscale that particular function independently, preventing bottlenecks elsewhere.

4. **Error Handling and DLQs** Each step in a Sequence is backed by an underlying Channel and Subscription, which means it inherits Knative's event transport-level retries. If a service fails to process an event, Knative will retry delivery based on the delivery.retry and backoffDelay settings in the Subscription. However, application-level failures (e.g., DB timeouts, transient API errors) should be handled inside the function itself. If an event continues to fail despite Knative's retries, it is routed to a Dead Letter Queue (DLQ) for manual review or reprocessing.

5. **Observability** Knative integrates with tracing and logging tools such as OpenTelemetry, Jaeger, and Prometheus. This distributed tracing allows you to follow an event's journey through the entire chain. If something goes wrong, or if performance is lagging in a particular step, you have clear visibility into where to focus your troubleshooting.

Altogether, the Sequence resource ties together Knative Services in a logical flow, abstracting away the inter-service communication. You define the order of execution once, and Knative automatically handles the restscaling, routing, retries, and even distributed tracing. This makes it significantly easier to implement and operate complex multi-step workflows without reinventing orchestration each time. In essence, Knative Sequence provides a powerful abstraction for function chaining, handling the intricate details of event routing, reliability, and observability, allowing developers to focus on the core business logic of each step.

Benefits of Using Knative

The benefits of using Knative for implementing the Function Chaining pattern are numerous and directly address common challenges in building complex serverless workflows. Knative's design philosophy is centered around simplifying the developer experience and providing robust operational capabilities, making it an ideal choice for advanced orchestration. Here are key advantages:

- **Simplified Development**: Knative abstracts away the complexities of workflow orchestration. Developers can focus on writing modular, reusable functions, while Knative takes care of routing events, managing dependencies, and ensuring reliability.

- **Scalability**: Functions scale independently using Auto-scaling. As discussed in Chapter 6, developers can write simple, stateless functions without worrying about provisioning or scaling infrastructure, as Knative handles it seamlessly.

- **Enhanced Observability**: Integrated observability tools, such as distributed tracing and logging, empower developers to gain real-time insights into their workflows. This reduces debugging time and improves the overall developer experience.

- **Cost Efficiency**: By auto-scaling services only when needed, Knative minimizes resource usage, enabling developers to optimize costs while maintaining performance.

By leveraging Knative, the Function Chaining Pattern becomes more robust and production-ready, aligning perfectly with modern cloud-native practices. This workflow not only enhances customer experience but also demonstrates the power of event-driven systems.

9.1.2 Parallel & Conditional Flows

While Sequences work well for strictly ordered workflows, many real-world applications require more flexible orchestration. For example, you might need to:

- **Fan out** an event to multiple subscribers, running tasks in parallel.

- **Filter** or conditionally branch based on event attributes (e.g., event type, priority, or user role).

- **Merge (fan-in)** or coordinate the outcomes of parallel branches.

Knative provides a *Parallel* resource (similar to Sequence) to address these scenarios. By defining multiple branches, each with an optional filter and a subscriber, you can execute tasks in parallel or route events based on attributes or custom logic.

Knative Parallel Overview

A **Parallel** object is conceptually similar to a Sequence, but instead of chaining steps linearly, it branches an event to multiple consumers simultaneously (or conditionally). Each branch can either handle the *same* event or only those matching specific criteria. After processing, you can optionally merge the branch outputs or send them to a final destination using the `reply` section.

Key elements of a `Parallel` resource include:

- **channelTemplate**: Defines the messaging channel used for internal routing (e.g., `InMemoryChannel`, `KafkaChannel`).

- **branches**: An array of branches. Each branch can specify:

    - **filter** (optional): A set of attribute-based filters. If specified, only events matching these filters are routed to that branch.

    - **subscriber**: The Knative Service (or addressable endpoint) that processes the event in that branch.

- **reply** (optional): Specifies where the outputs from each branch should go if you want to fan-in or collect results into another service or channel.

Similar to Sequences, the 'Parallel' resource also uses a 'channelTemplate'. This again offers the power of abstraction. By configuring the 'channelTemplate', you determine the underlying channel implementation (e.g., 'InMemoryChannel', 'KafkaChannel') that Knative uses to manage event routing between the branches of the Parallel flow. This allows you to tailor the messaging infrastructure to your specific requirements for durability, scalability, and performance, as detailed in

(Chapter 8) .

Simple Parallel Flows (Fan-Out)

Fan-out refers to sending the *same event* to multiple subscribers simultaneously, without filtering. This is the simplest form of parallel processing: one event fans out to multiple tasks.

Below is a minimal example of a `Parallel` resource that runs two services — inventory-service and analytics-service — in parallel for every incoming event. The inventory service updates the inventory, while the analytics service logs the inventory change for analysis.

```
1  apiVersion: flows.knative.dev/v1
2  kind: Parallel
3  metadata:
4    name: inventory-update-parallel
5  spec:
6    channelTemplate:
7      apiVersion: messaging.knative.dev/v1
8      kind: InMemoryChannel
9    branches:
10     - subscriber:
11         ref:
12           apiVersion: serving.knative.dev/v1
13           kind: Service
14           name: inventory-service
15     - subscriber:
16         ref:
17           apiVersion: serving.knative.dev/v1
18           kind: Service
19           name: analytics-service
```

Listing 9.2: Knative Parallel for Fan-Out

In this fan-out scenario:

- Both `inventory-service` and `analytics-service` receive each incoming event.

- No filters are applied, so the same event is processed by both branches.

Use Cases

- Multiple Independent Tasks: If you want to update inventory and log analytics data in parallel whenever an event arrives.

- Parallel Notifications: Send an order confirmation email to the user and a Slack notification to an internal channel.

Adding Filters for Conditional Branches

If you want to *selectively route* events to different branches, you can add filter rules. Currently, Knative Parallel primarily supports attribute-based filters, as demonstrated in the examples. This allows you to filter events based on CloudEvent attributes like 'type', 'source', or custom attributes you add. While attribute-based filtering is powerful for many conditional routing scenarios, it's worth noting that for more complex filtering logic — perhaps involving the event data itself or external systems — you might need to employ code-based routing in a preceding Knative Service. We'll touch upon this briefly later in this section when discussing advanced logic.

For example, an e-commerce platform might process EVENT_ORDER_PLACED events differently based on a `priority` attribute. The following YAML demonstrates how to **filter** events for each branch:

```
apiVersion: flows.knative.dev/v1
```

```
 2 kind: Parallel
 3 metadata:
 4   name: order-processing-parallel
 5 spec:
 6   channelTemplate:
 7     apiVersion: messaging.knative.dev/v1
 8     kind: InMemoryChannel
 9   branches:
10     - filter:
11         attributes:
12           priority: "high"
13       subscriber:
14         ref:
15           apiVersion: serving.knative.dev/v1
16           kind: Service
17           name: priority-order-service
18     - filter:
19         attributes:
20           priority: "standard"
21       subscriber:
22         ref:
23           apiVersion: serving.knative.dev/v1
24           kind: Service
25           name: standard-order-service
26   reply:
27     ref:
28       apiVersion: serving.knative.dev/v1
29       kind: Service
30       name: order-reply-logger
```

Listing 9.3: Knative Parallel with Attribute Filters

Here:

- **priority-order-service** handles high-priority orders, perhaps expediting fulfillment or sending special notifications.

- **standard-order-service** handles standard orders in a more routine fashion.

- While both branches might receive the same event, filters ensure the each branch only processes events matching its specific criteria ... `priority=high` or `priority=standard`.

- A reply destination (`order-reply-logger`) can fan-in the outputs from both branches (e.g., to log them, or further transform the result).

Fan-In and Advanced Logic You can also *fan-in* the results of multiple branches by specifying a `reply` destination. Once each branch completes and sends its outputevent, the `reply` service (or channel) receives and merges (or logs)those parallel outcomes before proceeding. For more complex scenarios, an *upstream function* may enrich the CloudEvent with attributes (e.g.,`membership=premium`), so downstream branches can filter on that value.Alternatively, you might use *code-based routing* to direct events to `branchA-channel` or `branchB-channel` based on business logic in your function, rather than relying solely on attribute filters in YAML. For scenarios requiring very fine-grained filtering or logic beyond simple attribute matching, this programmatic approach offers more flexibility, although it does require more code in your routing services.

When to Use Parallel or Conditional Flows

- **Concurrent Tasks**: Running tasks in parallel can drastically reduce total latency if the tasks are independent (e.g., analytics, notifications, billing).

- **Branching Based on Event Data**: Some events may need specialized handling (e.g., orders under $50 vs. orders over $50, or priority vs. standard).

- **Simplifying Service Logic**: Instead of embedding conditional flow inside a single monolithic function, you can keep each path's logic in its own service, making the system more modular and testable.

- **Dynamic Routing Needs**: If your event flows change frequently, using Parallel with filters can be more flexible than rewriting code-based conditionals.

Choosing to implement parallel or conditional flows using Knative Parallel offers significant advantages in terms of performance, modularity, and adaptability, particularly when compared to monolithic, conditionally complex functions. By leveraging Knative's built-in event routing and filtering capabilities, you can design more flexible, scalable, and maintainable event-driven systems. By combining these branching options with robust error handling (DLQs, retries) and auto-scaling, you can build sophisticated, event-driven applications that adapt to evolving business needsall while maintaining high reliability and clear observability.

9.2 Event Schema and Versioning

In previous chapters, we noted that one of the biggest challenges in event-driven systems is evolving the *structure* of events over time without disrupting existing consumers. Knative Eventing relies on the CloudEvents specification (Chapter 8), which promotes a standardized set of metadata (such as specversion, type, source, etc.) to ensure interoperability. In a serverless world, event producers and consumers are often managed by different teams, making synchronized updates difficult. Remember, events form a contract between producers and consumers. The **data payload** which often reflects domain-specific business requirements, must be designed to accommodate changes gracefully.

As systems grow and requirements evolve, new features or changes to business logic often necessitate updates to event schemas. In our e-commerce platform we store new metadata about orders (e.g., loyalty points, delivery preferences). If you simply add new fields to the data object, consumers that expect the old format might break. Conversely, older consumers might ignore the new fields and carry on, leading to inconsistent data flows. Evolving event schemas without a plan can lead to significant issues:

- **Maintaining Backward and Forward Compatibility**: Ensures that existing consumers continue to function without requiring immediate updates, and that new consumers can process older events if needed.

- **Reducing Deployment Risks and Operational Complexity**: Allows for incremental rollout of new features and easier debugging by verifying that existing workflows remain unaffected. Schema changes without a strategy can increase operational overhead.

- **Supporting Multiple Versions and Independent Scalability**: Different teams or microservices may operate at different paces, requiring support for various event payload versions. A sound strategy enables independent scaling of producers and consumers.

- **Data Integrity**: Prevents data corruption or misinterpretation, which is crucial for maintaining the accuracy of business decisions based on event data.

Therefore, a proactive strategy for schema evolution is not merely a best practice, but a necessity for building and maintaining resilient and long-lived event-driven systems.

9.2.2 Strategies for Schema Evolution

A well-defined strategy for schema evolution can help mitigate these challenges. Below are some common approaches:

Versioned Event Types

Versioning the `type` attribute in CloudEvents provides explicit differentiation between schema versions. THis is done by embedding the version within the CloudEvent's `type` attribute. For example:

- `order.created.v1` represents the initial event schema.

- `order.created.v2` for the revised schema with additional fields.

This strategy allows consumers to explicitly subscribe to compatible versions based on the `type`. It simplifies breaking changes by isolating them to specific versions. This approach is often easiest when changes are substantial or potentially breaking. However, it requires producers to manage multiple versions simultaneously and increases the complexity of consumer subscription configurations

Example: Versioned Events

```
1  {
2    "specversion": "1.0",
3    "type": "order.created.v1",
4    "source": "/ecommerce/orders",
```

```
 5    "id": "12345",
 6    "time": "2023-12-01T12:00:00Z",
 7    "data": {
 8      "order_id": "12345",
 9      "customer_id": "user-1001",
10      "total_amount": 150.00,
11      "loyalty_points": 15
12    }
13 }
```

Listing 9.4: Versioned Order Created Event

Backward-Compatible Changes

If your change is additive (e.g., introducing a new optional field), design your code so that older consumers ignore unknown fields. This means:

- Mark new fields as optional with sensible defaults.

- Avoid removing or renaming existing fields unless you create a new version.

Expand and Contract Pattern (Parallel Change)

This robust pattern involves:

1. **Expand**: Introduce a new event structure alongside the old one (e.g., new field or event type).

2. **Migrate**: Update consumers to use the new structure.

3. **Contract**: Remove the old structure after all consumers have migrated.

These strategies, when thoughtfully applied, provide a toolkit for managing schema evolution in event-driven systems, minimizing disruption and ensuring continued interoperability between producers and consumers.

9.2.3 Example: Evolving the Order Event

Lets look at an example of evolving the Order.created schema to include delivery preferences below.

Version 1:

```
1  {
2    "specversion": "1.0",
3    "type": "order.created.v1",
4    "source": "/ecommerce/orders",
5    "id": "12345",
6    "time": "2023-12-01T12:00:00Z",
7    "datacontenttype": "application/json",
8    "data": {
9      "order_id": "12345",
10     "customer_id": "user-1001",
11     "total_amount": 150.00
12   }
13 }
```

Listing 9.5: Order Created Event (v1)

Version 2 (with delivery_preferences):

```
1  {
2    "specversion": "1.0",
3    "type": "order.created.v2",
```

```
 4    "source": "/ecommerce/orders",
 5    "id": "67890",
 6    "time": "2023-12-05T14:30:00Z",
 7    "datacontenttype": "application/json",
 8    "data": {
 9      "order_id": "67890",
10      "customer_id": "user-2002",
11      "total_amount": 200.00,
12      "delivery_preferences": {
13        "priority": "express",
14        "address_type": "office"
15      }
16    }
17 }
```

Listing 9.6: Order Created Event (v2)

We can now create a Knative Trigger for the new `order.created.v2` event type. This ensures that the updated event is routed to the correct consumer service. The existing `order-processor` service can continue to handle the original `order.created.v1` events, while a new `order-processor-v2` service processes the updated events.

Knative Trigger for `order.created.v2`:

```
 1  apiVersion: eventing.knative.dev/v1
 2  kind: Trigger
 3  metadata:
 4    name: order-created-v2-trigger
 5  spec:
 6    broker: default
 7    filter:
 8      attributes:
 9        type: order.created.v2
10    subscriber:
11      ref:
12        apiVersion: serving.knative.dev/v1
13        kind: Service
14        name: order-processor-v2
```

Listing 9.7: Knative Trigger for v2 Events

This versioning example showcases a practical approach to evolving event schemas within Knative Eventing, leveraging Triggers to route different event versions to appropriate handlers, maintaining system stability during evolution. Effective schema evolution ensures that as your business grows, your event-driven system remains flexible, reliable, and easy to maintain.

Now that we've established best practices for schema evolution, let's explore how Knative handles event delivery reliability. Even with versioned schemas, failures are inevitable — services might be down, messages could be lost, or incorrect schemas could cause rejections. In the next section, we will look at strategies to ensure robust event delivery, including retries and Dead Letter Queues.

9.3 Handling Failure Scenarios

In any distributed system, failures are inevitable. A robust orchestration platform must provide mechanisms to handle these failures gracefully, and Knative Eventing excels in this area. Knative Eventing provides several mechanisms to handle such failures gracefully:

- **Retries**: Ensure temporary failures (e.g., network glitches, slow downstream services) are retried with a configurable **backoff policy**.

- **Dead Letter Queues (DLQs)**: Capture **undelivered events** for reprocessing and debugging.

- **Circuit Breakers**: Prevent cascading failures by temporarily halting event delivery to failing services.

9.3.1 Retries and Backoff Strategies

Resilience is a core tenet of Knative Eventing, and its built-in retry mechanisms are a prime example. By default, Knative Eventing attempts to **retry failed event deliveries** before sending them to a DLQ. You can configure:

- **Max Retries**: Limits how many times an event should be retried before marking it as failed.

- **Backoff Policies**: Controls **delay between retries**. Options include:

  - **Linear** (constant delay)

  - **Exponential** (increasing delay per attempt)

  - **Jittered** (randomized delays to prevent retry storms)

Example: Configuring Retries

The following configuration ensures that **failed events are retried up to 3 times with a 10-second delay** before being sent to the DLQ.

```
apiVersion: eventing.knative.dev/v1
kind: Broker
metadata:
  name: payment-broker
spec:
```

```
 6   delivery:
 7     retry: 3
 8     backoffPolicy: linear
 9     backoffDelay: PT10S
10     deadLetterSink:
11       ref:
12         apiVersion: serving.knative.dev/v1
13         kind: Service
14         name: dlq-service
```

Listing 9.8: Knative Broker configuration with retry and DLQ

When to Use Retries

- If failures are **temporary** (e.g., momentary service unavailability).

- If services are **idempotent** (i.e., retrying does not cause duplicate processing issues).

- If you want to **minimize DLQ usage** by giving services a chance to recover.

Retries, when configured appropriately with backoff strategies, become a crucial first line of defense against transient failures in event delivery, enhancing the overall reliability of the system.

9.3.2 Circuit Breakers: Preventing Retry Storms

While Knative Eventing provides built-in retries with backoff policies, persistent failures can lead to retry storms, where failing events are continuously retried, overwhelming a struggling service. This is particularly problematic when a service is under heavy load or experiencing degraded performance. While Knative Eventing provides built-in retries with backoff policies, persistent failures can lead to retry storms. It's crucial to understand that the circuit breaker functionality described in this section relies on Istio, a service mesh, being deployed and configured within your Kubernetes cluster where Knative is running. If you are not using Istio, these specific circuit breaker configurations will not be applicable. However, the general concept of circuit breaking for resilience is still highly relevant, and you might explore other circuit breaker implementations if you are not using Istio. For users not employing Istio, alternative circuit breaker implementations exist, such as those provided by libraries within your application code (e.g., Resilience4j for Java) or potentially through other Kubernetes-native solutions. Exploring these options is recommended for robust failure handling. In **Knative deployments that use Istio**, you can apply **circuit breaker policies** to temporarily halt retries when failures exceed a certain threshold. This prevents an already-failing service from being flooded with new requests, allowing it time to recover.

For example, you can configure Istio to:

- **Limit concurrent requests** to a failing Knative Service.

- **Temporarily reject new traffic** if failure rates exceed a defined threshold.

- **Gradually restore traffic** once the service stabilizes.

This approach ensures that Knative Eventing retries remain helpful rather than harmful, providing a balance between resilience and system stability.

How Circuit Breakers Work:

1. If a service **fails too many times**, the circuit breaker **opens**, temporarily stopping retries.

2. After a **cooldown period**, it attempts **one** event delivery to check if the service has recovered.

3. If successful, normal retries resume. If not, it **stays open** to avoid overloading the failing service.

Circuit breakers offer a critical safeguard against retry storms and cascading failures, ensuring that retries remain a beneficial resilience mechanism rather than a source of system instability during prolonged outages.

Example: Circuit Breaker Configuration (Istio + Knative)

This example demonstrates how to configure an Istio `DestinationRule` to apply a circuit breaker policy to a Knative Service named payment-service. Remember, this configuration is specifically for Istio and assumes Istio is managing traffic within your Knative cluster. If Istio is not present, this `DestinationRule` will have no effect.

```
apiVersion: networking.istio.io/v1alpha3
kind: DestinationRule
metadata:
  name: payment-service
spec:
  host: payment-service.default.svc.cluster.local
  trafficPolicy:
    connectionPool:
      http:
        maxRetries: 3
    outlierDetection:
      consecutiveErrors: 5
      interval: 10s
      baseEjectionTime: 30s
```

Listing 9.9: Istio DestinationRule for Circuit Breaker on Knative Service

This configuration automatically blocks event delivery to payment-service if it fails **5 times within 10 seconds**, preventing excess retries.

9.3.3 Dead Letter Queues (DLQs)

Retries cannot recover from all failures. If a service is permanently down, or an event is malformed, Knative Eventing routes failed events to a DLQ for later inspection. When an event is routed to a DLQ, it is essentially sent as a CloudEvent to the 'deadLetterSink' service you configure in your Broker (or Channel) definition. This deadLetterSink is typically a Knative Service (as shown in the examples), but it could also be any addressable endpoint that can accept CloudEvents. Common implementations for dlq-service include services that log events to durable storage (like a database or object storage) for later inspection and analysis.

Knative Eventing itself doesn't provide automated reprocessing of DLQ events. Reprocessing is typically a manual or out-of-band operation. Teams might build separate tools or processes to monitor the DLQ service's logs, analyze failed events, and then potentially resubmit events back into the eventing system after identifying and resolving the root cause of the failure. The specifics of reprocessing are highly application-dependent and often involve custom tooling. Furthermore, as discussed in Chapter 3 in the context of error handling in event-driven architectures, a well-designed system often includes dedicated error handler functions that are triggered by events arriving in the DLQ. These functions can implement specific error handling logic, such as logging, notifications, retry mechanisms, or compensatory actions.

Example: Payment Failure Handling with DLQ

If a payment service is unreachable despite 3 retry attempts, the event is stored in a `DLQ service` for later analysis.

```
 1  apiVersion: eventing.knative.dev/v1
 2  kind: Broker
 3  metadata:
 4    name: payment-broker
 5  spec:
 6    delivery:
 7      retry: 3
 8      backoffPolicy: exponential
 9      backoffDelay: PT5S
10      deadLetterSink:
11        ref:
12          apiVersion: serving.knative.dev/v1
13          kind: Service
14          name: dlq-service
```

Listing 9.10: Knative Broker Configuration with Dead Letter Queue

[Why DLQs Matter:]

- Ensure **no events are lost**, even when services fail.

- Allow for **manual recovery** (e.g., replaying events after fixing a bug).

- Help **debug failures effectively** (tracing failed events back to the source).

Dead Letter Queues, while representing failed event deliveries, provide an essential mechanism for capturing and analyzing persistent failures, enabling teams to diagnose issues and improve the overall robustness of their event-driven architectures.

9.4 Observability and Debugging

As emphasized in Chapter 7, debugging distributed, event-driven systems can be challenging due to asynchronous communication and multiple independent services. Knative Eventing provides hooks for comprehensive observability to address these challenges.

In today's complex, distributed systems, particularly those built on serverless and event-driven architectures, observability is paramount. The loosely coupled nature of Knative applications, while offering flexibility and scalability, makes it challenging to understand the flow of events and pinpoint the root cause of issues. Observability provides the means to understand the internal state of a system based on its external outputs, allowing you to effectively debug, monitor, and optimize its behavior, even in complex asynchronous environments. Knative addresses this challenge by embracing the three pillars of observability: **logs**, **metrics**, and **distributed tracing**. These pillars, along with tools like Prometheus, Grafana, Jaeger, and centralized logging systems, were introduced in Chapter 5 in the context of Knative Serving. In this chapter, we will delve deeper into how these observability pillars and tools are specifically applied and leveraged within Knative Eventing to understand and debug event-driven workflows.

- **Logs**: Detailed logs of each function's execution, correlated by event IDs or trace IDs. Logs provide granular, event-level information about what happened within each service. In an event-driven system, structured logs, as we will discuss, are crucial for correlating activities across different services based on event flow.

- **Metrics**: Aggregated data about system performance, such as throughput, latency, and error rates. As explored in Chapter 5, metrics provide quantitative, aggregated data about system performance and health over time. In Eventing, key metrics include event delivery counts, retry rates, and processing latencies, allowing you to monitor the overall health and efficiency of your event flows.

- **Tracing**: End-to-end tracing to see how events traverse your entire system. Distributed tracing is especially critical in event-driven architectures. It enables you to follow the journey of a single event as it propagates through multiple services, providing a holistic view of the entire transaction and helping to pinpoint bottlenecks or failures across service boundaries.

9.4.1 Logs and Correlation IDs

Each Knative Service generates its own logs, typically through standard output (stdout) and standard error (stderr) in the container. Knative automatically adds `ce-` prefixed attributes to CloudEvents, such as `ce-traceid`, `ce-id`, `ce-source`, and `ce-type`, which are invaluable for correlating logs across services.

To effectively manage logs in a distributed environment:

- **Use Structured Logging**: Adopt a structured logging format, such as JSON, to make logs machine-readable and easily queryable. Include the `ce-traceid` (or a custom trace ID) in every log entry.

  Example of a structured log entry:

```
1  {
2      "timestamp": "2023-12-20T10:00:00Z",
3      "severity": "INFO",
4      "message": "Order processed successfully",
5      "service": "order-processor",
6      "trace_id": "f47ac10b-58cc-4372-a567-0e02b2c3d479",
7      "order_id": "12345"
8  }
```

9

Listing 9.11: Structured Log Entry

- **Leverage a Log Aggregation System**: Tools like the **ELK Stack** (Elasticsearch, Logstash, Kibana), **Fluentd + Grafana Loki**, Splunk, or Datadog can ingest logs from all your Knative services into a central location. This makes it possible to trace a single event's journey across multiple services using its correlation ID.

- **Utilize Log Levels**: Employ appropriate log levels (DEBUG, INFO, WARNING, ERROR, CRITICAL) to categorize log entries by severity. This helps filter logs and focus on relevant information during debugging.

9.4.2 Metrics for System Health

Metrics provide quantitative insights into your system's performance and health. Knative exposes metrics in a Prometheus-friendly format, supporting a pull-based model. This means that Prometheus periodically scrapes (pulls) metrics from Knative components, as opposed to Knative pushing metrics to a central collector.

Prometheus Integration Knative exposes metrics related to both Knative Serving (e.g., request count, latency, concurrency) and Knative Eventing (e.g., event delivery count, processing time). You can also define and expose your own custom application-level metrics. To get most from it you need to understand:

- **Push vs Pull**: While Knative uses a pull based model, it is useful to understand when one might consider the alternative.

- **Cardinality**: Metrics with high cardinality can impact performance and should be used with care

Commonly monitored metrics include:

- **Event Delivery Count**: The number of events received by each service or channel.

- **Retry Attempts**: The frequency of retries, indicating potential transient errors.

- **Auto-scaling Behavior**: How quickly Knative Serving scales up or down based on load.

- **Request Latency**: The time taken to process a request (for Knative Services).

- **Error Rates**: The percentage of failed requests or event processing attempts.

Grafana Dashboards Grafana is often used to visualize Prometheus metrics. Create dashboards that display:

- **Latency Histograms**: Distributions of latencies for each service or function, helping identify performance bottlenecks.

- **Error Rate Over Time**: Graphs showing error rates, allowing you to quickly spot spikes that might indicate problems.

- **Resource Utilization**: CPU and memory usage of Knative Service pods, helping optimize resource allocation.

9.4.3 Distributed Tracing

Distributed tracing provides a holistic view of how requests or events propagate through your system. Knative supports injecting trace headers into CloudEvents, enabling end-to-end tracing. OpenTelemetry has emerged as the standard for distributed tracing and observability.

OpenTelemetry + Jaeger/Zipkin

Knative supports injecting trace headers into CloudEvents, allowing you to:

1. **Propagate a Trace Context**: So each function that receives the event logs the same `trace id`.

2. **View a Trace Timeline**: Tools like Jaeger or Zipkin show each span or step in the flow (Sequence or Parallel branches).

3. **Identify Bottlenecks**: If a step consumes significantly more time or fails often, the trace map reveals it quickly.

When an event is first emitted (e.g., `EVENT_ORDER_PLACED`), assign it a trace ID. Subsequent steps in the chain or parallel branches automatically attach logs and metrics to that same ID. This correlation makes debugging a multi-service flow as straightforward as following a single thread of execution across asynchronous boundaries.

9.4.4 Debugging Strategy: Leveraging Observability

Now that we have a good understanding of how traces are generated and how Knative implements observability through logs, metrics, and tracing, we can effectively leverage these tools to diagnose and resolve issues in our event-driven applications. When a problem arises, follow these steps to pinpoint the root cause:

- **1. Start with a Trace**: Your first step should be to examine the distributed trace associated with the failing or problematic event. Use Jaeger or Zipkin to visualize the event's path through your system. The trace provides a high-level overview, allowing you to quickly identify:

    - **Which services were involved?**: The trace shows the sequence of services that processed the event.

    - **Where did the failure occur?**: Failed spans are usually visually highlighted (e.g., in red) in the trace view, indicating the point of failure.

    - **Which operations were slow?**: The duration of each span is displayed, revealing potential performance bottlenecks.

- **2. Check Dead Letter Queues (DLQs)**: If the event failed to be processed successfully by a service, it might have been routed to a configured Dead Letter Queue (DLQ).

    - **Inspect the DLQ**: Examine the events in the DLQ to find the one related to your trace ID.

    - **Analyze Error Information**: DLQ events often contain error details explaining why the event couldn't be processed. This information can provide valuable clues about the nature of the problem. Furthermore, as discussed in Chapter 3 in the context of error handling in event-driven architectures, a well-designed system often includes dedicated error handler functions that are triggered by events arriving in the DLQ. These functions can implement specific error handling logic, such as logging, notifications, retry mechanisms, or compensatory actions.

- **3. Examine Logs**: With the trace ID and the potential point of failure identified, delve into your log aggregation system.

  - **Correlate Logs with Trace ID**: Use the `trace id` from the trace or `event id` from the CloudEvent as a filter in your logging tool to find all log entries related to the event.

  - **Analyze Log Details**: Examine the logs from the services involved in the trace, particularly those around the time of the failure or slow operation. Look for error messages, warnings, exceptions, or any unusual activity that could shed light on the issue.

  - **Utilize Structured Logging**: This is where structured logging becomes invaluable, allowing you to easily filter and query logs based on specific fields (e.g., `service`, `order_id`, etc.).

- **4. Analyze Metrics**: Metrics provide insights into the system's health and performance around the time of the problem.

  - **Look for Anomalies**: Check your Grafana dashboards (or other metric visualization tools) for spikes in error rates, latency, or resource utilization (CPU, memory) in the services identified by the trace.

- **Correlate with Trace Timeline**: Compare the timestamps of metric anomalies with the timeline of the trace to see if they coincide. This can help establish a causal link between the observed metrics and the event's failure or slow processing.

- **Identify Resource Bottlenecks**: High resource utilization might indicate resource exhaustion (e.g., insufficient CPU or memory), while increased latency could point to slow dependencies or network issues.

- **5. Review Error Handling**: Once you have a better understanding of the problem, examine the error handling logic in your code.

  - **Are exceptions handled gracefully?** Verify that your services have appropriate 'try-catch' blocks or other error-handling mechanisms to catch and handle exceptions without crashing.

  - **Is error information propagated usefully?** Ensure that error messages are informative and that relevant context (like the event id or relevant data from the event) is logged or propagated to aid in debugging.

  - **Are retries implemented correctly?** If your services use retries, make sure they are configured with appropriate backoff strategies and retry limits to avoid exacerbating the problem.

- **6. Reproduce the Issue**: To effectively debug and test potential fixes, try to reproduce the issue in a controlled environment.

  - **Local Debugging**: If possible, reproduce the issue locally using a debugger to step through the code and inspect variables.

- **Staging Environment**: If local reproduction is not feasible, try to reproduce the issue in a staging environment that closely mirrors your production setup. This allows you to test fixes without impacting production users.

- **7. Set Up Alerts**: To proactively identify and address similar issues in the future, configure alerts based on metrics and logs.

  - **Metric-Based Alerts**: Create alerts that trigger when key metrics exceed defined thresholds (e.g., error rate above 5%, latency above 500ms).

  - **Log-Based Alerts**: Set up alerts that trigger when specific error messages or log patterns are detected.

By systematically combining the power of distributed tracing, correlated logs, and insightful metrics, you can transform the debugging process from a daunting task into a manageable and efficient investigation. This approach minimizes guesswork and allows you to quickly pinpoint the root cause of issues, even in complex, asynchronous, and distributed event-driven systems built on Knative.

9.4.5 Knative Observability Configuration

Knative's observability settings are primarily managed through ConfigMaps:

- **Knative Eventing:** The `config-observability` ConfigMap in the `knative-eventing` namespace allows you to configure logging, tracing, and request metrics settings for Knative Eventing components.

- **Knative Serving:** The `config-observability` ConfigMap in the `knative-serving` namespace controls logging and metrics for Knative Serving. The `config-defaults` ConfigMap in the same namespace manages auto-scaling settings, including metrics used for scaling decisions.

9.4.6 Security Considerations

When implementing observability, be mindful of security:

- **Sensitive Data**: Avoid logging or tracing personally identifiable information (PII), credentials, or other sensitive data.

- **Access Control**: Secure access to your logging, metrics, and tracing systems to prevent unauthorized access to sensitive operational data.

By combining logs, metrics, and tracing, you minimize the guesswork needed to pinpoint the root cause of issues in a distributed environment.

9.4.7 Debugging Failures: Tracing & Observability

When an event reaches a **DLQ**, Knative automatically attaches **error metadata** such as:

- `knativeerrorcode`: The HTTP response status (e.g., `500` for internal errors).

- `knativeerrordata`: Details on why event delivery failed.

Use **Jaeger, Prometheus, and structured logs** to analyze failures:

Table 9.1: Debugging Tools for Knative Eventing Failures

Tool	Purpose	Example
Jaeger	Trace events **end-to-end** through the system	Find where an event got stuck using `event.id`. **Example:** In Jaeger UI, search by `event.id` to view the trace.
Prometheus	Monitor retry counts, DLQ spikes, and failures	Alert when `dlq_service` exceeds 10 events/min. **Example PromQL Query:** `rate(eventing_dlq_failure` > 10
Loki (Logs)	Correlate logs across services using `ce-traceid`	Find out why a specific payment event failed. `{app="payment-service"} | json | trace_id = "your-trace-id"`

Example: Debugging a Failed Payment Event

1. **Check Jaeger Tracing**

- Search for `event.id=abc123` and find where the event failed.

- If it hit a retry loop, check **service response times**.

2. **Query Prometheus Metrics**

   - `rate(eventing_dlq_failures[5m]) > 10` → Too many failures? Investigate.

3. **Review Structured Logs (Loki)**

   - Filter logs: `json | event.id == "abc123"`

   - Check `knativeerrorcode` (e.g., `400 Bad Request` → malformed event).

9.5 Multi-Tenant and Hybrid Environments

The increasing adoption of cloud-native architectures has led to a surge in **multi-tenant** and **hybrid cloud** deployments. **Multi-tenancy** involves multiple users, teams, or organizations sharing the same underlying infrastructure while maintaining isolation and security. **Hybrid cloud** combines on-premises systems with public cloud services, offering flexibility and control. Knative, with its serverless platform and event-driven capabilities, is particularly well-suited to address the complexities of these environments.

Namespace Isolation: Foundation of Multi-Tenancy

The cornerstone of multi-tenancy in Kubernetes is the concept of **namespaces**. Each tenant can operate within their own dedicated namespace, providing a logical boundary for resources. Within each namespace, you can deploy Knative resources like Brokers, Triggers, and Services, ensuring that events and workloads are isolated between tenants. This effectively creates separate, isolated Knative environments within the larger cluster. Within each namespace, tenants can deploy their Knative resources — **Services**, **Brokers**, **Triggers**, **Channels**, **Sources** — without worrying about naming conflicts or resource collisions with other tenants. For example, Tenant A can have a Knative Service named 'order-processor' in their namespace, and Tenant B can have a service with the same name in their own namespace without any issues. By deploying Brokers and Triggers within tenant-specific namespaces, you ensure that events are, by default, isolated to that tenant's environment. An event published to a Broker in Tenant A's namespace will only be delivered to Triggers and Services within that same namespace, unless explicitly configured otherwise. This prevents accidental or unauthorized cross-tenant event flow.Each tenant can configure their Knative resources independently, tailoring settings like auto-scaling parameters, event delivery options (e.g., retries, dead-letter queues), and even the choice of Channel implementation to their specific needs, all without affecting other tenants. From an operational perspective, namespaces simplify management tasks. For example, you can easily monitor resource usage, apply updates, or troubleshoot issues for a specific tenant by focusing on their dedicated namespace. Namespaces provide a natural boundary for applying security policies. As we'll discuss later, Kubernetes RBAC, Network Policies, and Pod Security mechanisms can be used to enforce fine-grained access control and network isolation at the namespace level, ensuring that tenants can only access and modify resources within their own environment.

Broker Strategies: Shared vs. Dedicated

While namespaces provide a strong foundation for isolating resources and events, the choice between deploying a shared Broker or dedicated Brokers per tenant remains relevant and introduces further considerations regarding the level of isolation, performance, management overhead, and security.

Shared Broker with Filtering A single, shared Broker can be deployed, and tenants can use **Knative Triggers** to filter events based on attributes like source, type, or custom attributes added to the CloudEvent. Events are processed by the shared broker but only delivered to Triggers that match the filter criteria within each namespace.

- **Pros**:

    - Potentially more resource-efficient, especially for numerous tenants with low or sporadic event traffic.

    - Simpler infrastructure management with a single Broker instance to monitor and maintain.

- **Cons**:

    - Requires careful configuration of Triggers to ensure proper event routing and prevent leakage between tenants.

    - The shared Broker could become a performance bottleneck under high load or a single point of failure.

    - Relies heavily on logical isolation provided by namespaces and security mechanisms like RBAC and Network Policies.

Not ideal for scenarios with stringent security requirements demanding physical separation.

Dedicated Brokers per Tenant   Each tenant namespace can have its own dedicated Knative Broker (or multiple Brokers). This creates a more physically isolated eventing infrastructure for each tenant.

- **Pros**:

    - Stronger isolation: Events are processed by separate Broker instances, minimizing the risk of cross-tenant interference.

    - Better performance isolation: One tenant's load won't impact others.

    - Easier to manage per tenant, as each tenant's eventing infrastructure is self-contained within their namespace.

    - Smaller blast radius: A failure in one tenant's Broker does not affect other tenants.

    - Enhanced security posture: Provides physical separation, which can be crucial for compliance with strict security regulations.

- **Cons**:

    - Might consume more resources, especially if many tenants have low event throughput.

    - Increased operational overhead from managing multiple Broker instances.

Trade-offs The choice between a shared or dedicated Broker strategy depends on the specific needs and priorities of your multi-tenant environment. While namespace-based isolation is fundamental, dedicated Brokers offer a higher degree of physical isolation, better performance guarantees, and a stronger security posture, making them generally preferred for scenarios with stringent security or compliance requirements, or when tenants have significant event traffic. Shared Brokers, on the other hand, can be more resource-efficient and easier to manage at scale when dealing with numerous tenants with lower event volumes, provided that careful attention is paid to Trigger configuration and security policies.

9.5.1 Securing Multi-Tenant Environments

While Knative Eventing simplifies event routing and management, production-grade multi-tenant deployments require careful consideration of security to ensure the isolation and integrity of each tenant's data and applications. This section outlines key security concerns and best practices for securing Knative Eventing in multi-tenant environments.

Authentication and Authorization: Securing Access to Resources

A robust security strategy starts with controlling who can access and modify resources within the cluster. Kubernetes provides mechanisms for both authentication (verifying the identity of users and applications) and authorization (determining what actions authenticated users are allowed to perform).

Role-Based Access Control (RBAC) Kubernetes Role-Based Access Control (RBAC) is a fundamental security mechanism that allows you to define granular permissions for users and applications based on their roles within the organization. In a multi-tenant Knative environment, RBAC plays a critical role in ensuring that each tenant can only manage resources within their designated namespace(s).

- **Service Accounts for Applications**: Each application or service running within a tenant's namespace should have a dedicated Kubernetes *ServiceAccount*. This ServiceAccount acts as the identity for the application when it interacts with the Kubernetes API or other services.

- **Namespaced Roles and RoleBindings**: Instead of granting cluster-wide permissions, define *Roles* within each tenant's namespace. These Roles specify the actions (e.g., get, list, create, update, delete) that are allowed on specific resources (e.g., Pods, Services, Knative Brokers, Triggers) within that namespace. Then, use *RoleBindings* to bind these Roles to the appropriate ServiceAccounts. This approach prevents tenants from accidentally or maliciously accessing or modifying other tenants' Knative resources, such as Brokers or Triggers, ensuring strong isolation.

```
1   apiVersion: rbac.authorization.k8s.io/v1
2   kind: Role
3   metadata:
4      namespace: tenant-a-namespace
5      name: tenant-a-knative-role
6   rules:
7   - apiGroups: ["eventing.knative.dev"]
8      resources: ["brokers", "triggers"]
9      verbs: ["get", "list", "watch", "create", "update",
    "patch", "delete"]
10  - apiGroups: ["serving.knative.dev"]
11     resources: ["services"]
12     verbs: ["get", "list", "watch", "create", "update",
    "patch", "delete"]
```

```
13    ---
14    apiVersion: rbac.authorization.k8s.io/v1
15    kind: RoleBinding
16    metadata:
17      name: tenant-a-knative-rolebinding
18      namespace: tenant-a-namespace
19    subjects:
20    - kind: ServiceAccount
21      name: tenant-a-service-account
22      namespace: tenant-a-namespace
23    roleRef:
24      kind: Role
25      name: tenant-a-knative-role
26      apiGroup: rbac.authorization.k8s.io
27
```

Listing 9.12: Example Role and RoleBinding for a Tenant

- **Principle of Least Privilege**: Adhere to the principle of least privilege. Grant only the minimum necessary permissions to each ServiceAccount. Avoid using overly permissive Roles or ClusterRoles unless absolutely required. Define granular policies for sensitive resources (e.g., Channels or Secrets).

- **ClusterRoles for Cluster-Wide Operations**: While most tenant operations should be restricted to their namespaces, there might be cases where limited cluster-wide access is needed. Use *ClusterRoles* and *ClusterRoleBindings* judiciously for such scenarios, ensuring that they are tightly scoped and only granted to trusted entities. For example a ClusterRole might be defined for read only access to a specific resource across all namespaces.

- **Regular Audits**: Use annotations and labels to enforce security workflows or audit controls per namespace. Regularly review and audit your RBAC policies to ensure they are up-to-date, accurate, and aligned with the principle of least privilege.

Authentication to the Kubernetes API Access to the Kubernetes API server should be secured using strong authentication mechanisms. Common methods include:

- **Service Account Tokens**: Automatically mounted into pods and used by applications to authenticate to the API server.

- **X.509 Client Certificates**: More secure than tokens, often used for external access or by administrators.

- **External Identity Providers (IdPs)**: Integrate with existing enterprise IdPs (e.g., LDAP, Active Directory, SAML providers) to centralize user management and leverage existing authentication infrastructure.

By implementing robust RBAC policies and securing API access, you can effectively prevent unauthorized access to Knative resources and ensure that each tenant can only operate within their designated boundaries. This approach prevents one tenant from accidentally (or maliciously) modifying another tenant's Knative resources, such as Brokers, Triggers or Services.

9.5.2 Orchestrating a Secure Multi-Tenant Future

Multi-tenant and hybrid deployments represent the new frontier of cloud-native architecture, offering compelling advantages in terms of resource efficiency, scalability, and flexibility. Organizations can empower teams to share infrastructure while seamlessly integrating on-premises systems with the agility of cloud services. Knative Eventing, with its serverless and event-driven nature, provides a powerful platform for building such complex applications. However, as we have empha-sized throughout this section, security must be a foundational design principle, not an afterthought.

Achieving a secure and robust multi-tenant and hybrid environment requires a multi-faceted approach:

- **Isolate with Confidence**: Leverage the bedrock of Kubernetes namespaces to create logically separated environments for each tenant. Combine this with granular Role-Based Access Control (RBAC) to enforce the principle of least privilege, and Network Policies to meticulously control traffic flow. This ensures that tenants can operate independently without any risk of accidental or malicious interference.

- **Encrypt Everything**: Protect data confidentiality both in transit and at rest. Employ TLS or mTLS to secure communication channels between services, whether they reside in the cloud or on-premises. If using persistent storage for events or state, ensure that the underlying storage mechanisms are encrypted.

- **Monitor Relentlessly**: Implement comprehensive monitoring and auditing across all layers of your system. Centralized logging, aggregated metrics, and distributed tracing provide the visibility needed to detect anomalies, identify security breaches, and troubleshoot issues effectively. Ensure that audit trails are in place to track all resource changes, especially in the shared Knative Eventing control plane.

- **Automate and Enforce Policies**: Utilize tools like Open Policy Agent (OPA)/Gatekeeper to define and automatically enforce security and compliance policies across your multi-tenant environment. This helps prevent misconfigurations and ensures that security best practices are consistently applied.

- **Embrace a Zero-Trust Mindset**: Assume that no user, service, or device should be inherently trusted. Implement strong authentication, authorization, and network security controls to verify the identity and permissions of every entity interacting with your system.

By diligently applying these principles and best practices, organizations can confidently run Knative Eventing in even the most demanding and sensitive multi-tenant and hybrid environments. You can achieve robust data protection, ensure regulatory compliance, and maintain operational integrity while still harnessing the power of event-driven, serverless architectures. Knative Eventing, when combined with a strong security posture, empowers you to build a future where agility, scalability, and security go hand in hand.

9.6 Summary

This chapter has demonstrated how advanced orchestration techniques, schema evolution strategies, and robust failure handling, all powered by Knative Eventing, allow you to realize the full potential of event-driven architectures. By moving beyond simple event routing and embracing these advanced concepts, you can build truly sophisticated, scalable, and resilient cloud-native systems. Systems where, as Aristotle observed, the whole is demonstrably greater than the sum of its parts. By leveraging these techniques:

- **Function Chaining** and **Sequences** enable multi-step processes that are easy to implement and maintain.

- **Resilient Failure Handling** (retries, backoff, DLQs) ensures robust recovery from transient outages or application errors.

- **Schema Evolution** strategies and **CloudEvents** best practices minimize breakage when event formats change.

- **Distributed Tracing and Metrics** provide the visibility needed to operate event-driven systems at scale.

- **Multi-Tenant and Hybrid** setups integrate seamlessly, allowing you to isolate users while bridging multiple environments.

By putting these advanced techniques into practice, you can build event-driven architectures that are ready for real-world complexityscalable, fault-tolerant, and adaptable to evolving business needs. This concludes our deep dive into Advanced Orchestration with Knative Eventing, bringing together the foundational EDA concepts from Chapter 7 and the fundamental Knative components from Chapter 8 into robust, end-to-end workflows. You are now well equipped to design and implement the kinds of large-scale, mission-critical systems that showcase the transformative power of EDA in the cloud, and specifically, the enabling power of Knative Eventing.

Epilogue: Embracing the Serverless Future

As we conclude our journey through the world of serverless computing and Knative, it's clear that we've only scratched the surface of this transformative technology. The serverless paradigm is not just about technology; it represents a cultural shift in how we approach scalability, resource management, and developer productivity. The landscape is constantly evolving, with new tools, frameworks, and best practices emerging all the time.

Throughout this book, we have explored the foundational concepts of serverless, examined practical patterns and architectures, and dived deep into Knative's capabilities. Along the way, we've seen how serverless can simplify the most complex workflows, empower developers to focus on innovation, and create applications that are truly elastic and efficient.

The adoption of serverless is more than a technical decision; it's a strategic move toward agility and resilience in an increasingly unpredictable digital landscape. By leveraging Knative's strengths on Kubernetes, you now have the tools to design and deploy systems that are not only robust but also future-proof.

But the story doesn't end here. The serverless ecosystem continues to evolve, with emerging trends like edge computing, AI/ML integrations, and hybrid cloud architectures redefining what's possible. Knative, with its open-source community and innovative features, is poised to lead this evolution.

As you embark on implementing what you've learned, remember that serverless is not just about achieving technical goals — it's about delivering value to your users with speed, reliability, and scale. Keep experimenting, keep innovating, and most importantly, keep building. I encourage you to stay abreast of newer developments and to continue experimenting with Knative and other serverless technologies. The future of cloud computing is serverless, and Knative is at the forefront of this movement.

I hope this book has provided you with a solid foundation for understanding and using Knative. I also hope it has inspired you to explore the endless possibilities of serverless computing.

The serverless future is bright, and I look forward to seeing what you build with Knative.

Thank you for joining me on this journey.

About the Author

Pradeep Loganathan is a cloud architect, software engineer, and technical speaker with extensive experience in serverless technologies, Kubernetes, and cloud-native development. Over the years, he has worked with enterprises to build scalable, secure, and efficient cloud architectures.

He has presented at international conferences, authored technical blogs, and contributed to open-source projects. Passionate about teaching and mentoring, Pradeep shares his knowledge through workshops, blogs, and public speaking engagements.

When he's not working on technology, Pradeep enjoys photography, riding motorcycles, and exploring different cuisines.

Website: https://pradeepl.com/
LinkedIn: https://linkedin.com/in/pradeeploganathan
Twitter: https://twitter.com/pradeepl